RAMBLERS' LEEDS

38 MOSTLY CIRCULAR WALKS WITH SKETCH MAPS

Compiled by

DOUGLAS COSSAR

for the Ramblers' Association (West Riding Area)

The Ramblers

Other publications by the Ramblers' Association (West Riding Area)

Ilkley Moor map & guide
Washburn Valley map & guide
Family Rambles around Bradford
Dales Way Handbook (with the Dales Way Association, annually)
West Yorkshire Rambles
More West Yorkshire Rambles
Kiddiwalks (new edition Spring 1995)

Ramblers' Leeds first published 1995

RAMBLERS' ASSOCIATION (WEST RIDING AREA)
27 Cookridge Avenue, Leeds LS16 7NA

ISBN 0 900613 82 3

Cover photograph: Autumn at Fulneck (Walk 25) (Valerie Magill)

Printed by Duffield Printers, Leeds

Publishers' Note

At the time of publication all footpaths used in these walks were designated as public rights of way or permissive footpaths, but it should be borne in mind that diversion orders may be made from time to time. Although every care has been taken in the preparation of this guide, neither the author nor the publisher can accept responsibility for those who stray from the routes described.

In memory of

Jack Madden, M.B.E.

in recognition of his tireless campaigns
in defence of the footpaths of Leeds

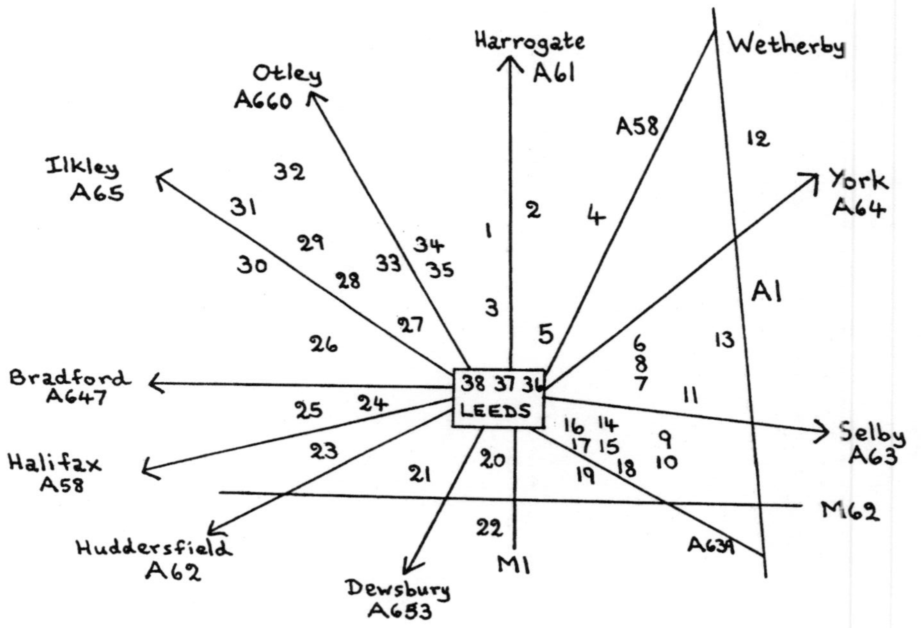

Harrogate A61
Wetherby
Otley A660
A58
12
Ilkley A65
York A64
32
31
2
4
1
29
34
30
33
35
28
A1
3
27
5
26
6
8
13
7
Bradford A647
38 37 36
LEEDS
11
24
25
16 14
23
17 15
9
Halifax A58
20
18
10
21
19
M62
22
A639
Huddersfield A62
M1
Dewsbury A653

Contents

The **Ramblers' Association**, a registered charity, is an organisation dedicated to the preservation and care of the countryside and its network of footpaths, and to helping people to appreciate and enjoy them.

Through its National Office the Ramblers' Association lobbies and campaigns for more effective legislation to achieve

- the preservation and improvement of the footpath network
- better access to the countryside
- the preservation and enhancement for the benefit of the public of the beauty of the countryside.

Since its formation in 1935 the Ramblers' Association has grown into a powerful campaigning organisation with a membership climbing towards 100,000.

The Association relies on many volunteers working at Area and Local Group level to help achieve these objectives.

The **West Riding Area** is one of the 51 Areas of the Ramblers' Association which cover England, Wales and Scotland. It includes the whole of West Yorkshire and parts of North Yorkshire around Selby, York, Harrogate, Ripon, Skipton and Settle, as well as the southern part of the Yorkshire Dales National Park. The Area has nearly 3,500 members and is divided into 13 Local Groups.

The **Local Groups** carry out the work of the Ramblers' Association by keeping an eye on the state of footpaths in their area and monitoring proposed closures and diversions.

- They put pressure on their Local Authority to take action to remove obstructions and re-instate footpaths after ploughing.
- They do practical work of footpath clearance and waymarking, and can erect stiles and footbridges.
- Where the Local Authority has set up consultation procedures, e.g. Footpath Forums, the Local Group will normally send a representative.
- Many Local Groups produce their own programme of walks.

Regular walks are a very important part of Ramblers' activities. As well as ensuring that local footpaths are used, they provide healthy recreation and the opportunity to make new friends.

If you use and enjoy the footpath network, please help us to protect it, by joining the Ramblers' Association. For further information write to the West Riding Area Membership Secretary

Mrs Dora Tattersall, 10 Woodvale Grove, Lidget Green, Bradford BD7 2SL, or to

The Ramblers' Association, 1/5 Wandsworth Road, London SW8 2XX.

Remember the Country Code:

Guard against all risk of fire.

Take your litter home. As well as being unsightly, it may be a hazard to livestock.

If you find a gate closed, be careful to close it again behind you. If it is open, leave it open.

Do not pollute streams or rivers, ponds, lakes or reservoirs.

Keep dogs under control: they may frighten other walkers or be a threat to livestock.

Protect, wildlife, plants and trees.

Keep to public paths across farmland.

Take special care on country roads.

Use gates and stiles to cross fences, hedges and walls.

Make no unnecessary noise.

Leave livestock, crops and machinery alone.

Enjoy the countryside and respect its life and work.

Jack Madden: an appreciation

Jack Madden led walks in all directions round Leeds, and the rambles in this book are on paths he knew well. All are accessible by public transport – I don't think Jack ever led a 'car ramble' in his life.

Jack was an active member of the Executive Committee of the West Riding Area of the Ramblers' Association for many years, and for much of that period he was also Chairman of the Leeds Group, diligently watching over our footpaths with loving care and fighting many noteworthy battles to preserve them – the famous protest walk along Miry Carr Lane at Thorner is an outstanding example.

But probably the achievement for which Jack will be most remembered was the creation of the Thursday group of walkers. He brought health and happiness to many pensioners, often lonely people living by themselves. He encouraged them and gave them confidence to take up walking. The Thursday group became a sort of club. There was a walk every week for most of the year, there were occasional coach rambles and of course a Christmas Dinner! Other leaders were brought in, to fill up an interesting and wide-ranging programme. The group became almost too popular – I remember leading about fifty walkers round Burley Moor. The 'Veterans', as they came to be called, were devoted to Jack – it was one of them who originated the idea that he should be awarded the M.B.E., and they insisted on dedicating their own memorial seat after his death (you can find it at Temple Newsam not far from the Mansion).

Jack was a lifelong walker. One of his favourite sayings was that unless you walk at all seasons and in all weathers you cannot claim to know the countryside. He certainly knew it – I remember him telling me how many orchids he had found in a particular lane near Harewood. But he had other interests as well – he used to spend Tuesdays painting at Swarthmore: some of the cover designs for the Leeds Group's magazine Gate 'n' Ginnel were based on his drawings. I understand that he had been an active trade unionist during his working life. A devout Catholic, he would go to church in the evening if he had set off walking too early in the morning – even though, as on one occasion I well remember, we had walked sixteen or seventeen miles.

Jack was a man who enriched the lives of many others, and this volume of rambles around Leeds is a small token of our gratitude and our affection.

Millie Benn

Author's note.

Leeds in the context of this book means the Metropolitan District of Leeds, and a substantial part of the route of each walk is within the Leeds District, although I have allowed myself to stray over the border from time to time for the sake of a more interesting ramble. I have tried to achieve a wide geographical spread of walks, but not all parts of Leeds are equally attractive to ramblers, and I'm afraid that some of my friends in South Leeds may feel that I have not done them justice! I hope that on the whole, however, the book represents reasonably well the variety and interest of the landscapes of Leeds. Those of us who live in and around the city have much to be grateful for.

All the paths used are definitive rights of way or permissive footpaths, and they are on the whole in much better shape now than they were when Jack Madden was active, thanks both to the vigilance and pressure of the Ramblers' Association and to the committed attitude of Leeds Leisure Services Countryside Service. If you should encounter any obstacles, obstructions, nuisances or other difficulties, please report them, either to the Footpaths Officer of the Leeds Group of the RA, Eric Barker, 16 Lulworth Avenue, Whitkirk, Leeds LS15 8LN, or to Leeds City Council's Rights of Way Section at Temple Newsam Home Farm, Leeds LS15 0BJ (Tel: 0113-232-6444). As a result of recent tragic accidents, dogs now seem generally to be kept under much better control than formerly, and indeed in the course of preparing this book there was only one occasion on which I was set upon by dogs. Look out for bulls at large in pastures in the summer months, and take suitable evasive action, even if this means a minor trespass. Better safe than sorry!

Writing a book of walks in and around a large city has taught me how much our environment is constantly changing, and our footpaths with it. New houses and housing estates are built, new roads appear and old ones are widened and upgraded, old coal mines are landscaped and become country parks, the course of canals and rivers is changed, not to mention the wear and tear on stiles and gates, fences and walls; and of course footpaths can be closed or diverted and new ones created. I hope that my descriptions are reasonably up to date, although I am aware that as a result of road-building projects soon to be carried out some of them may not be accurate for very long, and I am most grateful to Roger Brookes of the Rights of Way Section at Temple Newsam for reading the manuscript and for suggesting corrections and improvements. The final responsibility for the walks is of course my own.

All the walks can be located on the Ordnance Survey Landranger maps 104 (Leeds, Bradford & Harrogate) and 105 (York), and at the start of each walk I have given details of the relevant Pathfinder sheet(s). The sketch maps which accompany each walk are based on these Pathfinder maps and are reproduced with the permission of the Controller of H.M.S.O. They are intended to give an overview of the walk and to supplement the description, but as they are greatly simplified, particularly in built-up areas, they should not be used as a substitute for the description. Please read the descriptions carefully: I have tried to make them clear and unambiguous and to eliminate the risk of misinterpretation. I am sure you will let me know where I have failed! But in my experience lots of people go astray through not concentrating on the text of a walk, inadvertently skipping a line or jumping by mistake from one stile to the next, or just losing the place through being engrossed in conversation with their companions!

All the walks are accessible by public transport, and I have given details as they are known to me at the moment. But please do check this information with Leeds Metro for buses (Tel: 0113-245-7676) or British Rail for trains (Tel: 0113-244-8133).

I am grateful to all who have helped in the production of this book, especially Bruce McGreevy, Colin Newton and Hugh Thornton for checking a number of the descriptions. Any mistakes are of course my responsibility. Walk 35 is based on a suggestion by Joan Duffield. My gratitude also to Millie Benn for her appreciation of Jack Madden. Jack was one of my heroes when I first became active in footpath work for the Ramblers' Association, and I am proud to have been given this chance to produce a tribute to his achievements.

Douglas Cossar
December 1994

HAREWOOD CIRCULAR

WALK 1

5½ miles (9 km); Pathfinder 672 (SE24/34); an easy ramble almost entirely on tracks, partly through the parkland and woods of the Harewood Estate.

By bus: *No.36 Harrogate bus half-hourly from Leeds Central Bus Station. Alight at a gate on the left into the Harewood Estate, opposite a minor road to Wike on the right.*
By car: *Coming from Leeds on the A61 to Harrogate, shortly after the wall enclosing the Harewood estate begins on the left, there is a large wrought iron gate into the estate by a lodge, and opposite there is a minor road signposted to Wike. A few yards along this road there is a large layby with a memorial seat. Park here (GR 326 432).*

Return to the main road, cross and go through the righthand of the three large gates, then a wooden gate immediately after, and head along the track through the park. Immediately there is a fine view right to Harewood House and Lower Wharfedale. Pass through another two gates, and the track is now gently descending. Go through another gate and into the wood. Cross an 18th century stone bridge and bear left (bridleway sign). At the next fork keep right (signpost: you will note that you are on the Leeds Country Way). Shortly before you reach the end of the wood, with fields ahead, fork right at a junction of tracks (signpost) and cross the shallow valley of Stub House Beck. At the next crossing fork right (Ebor Way sign) on a descending track, soon coming to a T-junction where again you bear right downhill.

The track leads to a gate into a field, but 200 yards before this, fork left onto a narrower, descending path, which leads to the left of a stone barn, part of the derelict Carr House. Pass through the gate and keep forward down the track. The lake and the house are seen in the distance. Bear left at the next junction, and the track soon curves right to a gate. Pass to the left of an old walled garden. You are joined by a tarmac track from the right, and soon there is a fine view over Wharfedale to Weeton and Almscliff Crag. Drop to a crossroads: a short distance over the bridge on the right is Harewood House, but there is no right of way to it. Keep forward over another bridge then uphill through the Home Farm.

Cross a cattle-grid to re-enter the park. Cross another cattle-grid and walk forward to a junction (another nice view), where you bear right uphill. Cross another cattle-grid. The track on the right at this point leads to the mediaeval Harewood Parish Church, open every afternoon in summer and worth a visit, but our walk continues straight ahead to Harewood village. Keep forward to the main road, cross it (care!) and turn right, but only as far as the Harewood Arms. Immediately before the pub take the signposted path on the left, a tarmac lane. At the gate into Maltkiln House the lane bears slightly right, and when the tarmac ends go through the gate ahead and keep forward along the track with a small wood to the right (another fine view left over Wharfedale). Pass through another gate and immediately go right over a stile and walk down the righthand edge of the field to the A659 Harewood to Wetherby road.

Turn left along the road (there is a narrow footway). Shortly after passing a long layby and opposite a milepost take the access road on the right to New Laithe Farm. When the road forks just before the farm, keep left and pass round the lefthand end of the farmhouse onto a concrete track, and when this ends keep straight forward downhill with a hedge to your right to another gate. Keep forward down the next large field to a gate near the lefthand end of a row of tall trees. The gate is quickly followed by another one, and now you must bear slightly left uphill (no clear path) to the lefthand end of the buildings of Hollin Hall ahead. Pass to the left of the house, through a gate and straight downhill on a track to pass to the left of a lake. When you reach the wood bear right up to a gateway, then left on the track along the outside edge of the wood.

The track soon fades and now you must bear slightly right uphill away from the wood (there is a faint path) to a gate in the top lefthand corner of the field. Now there is a clear track up with the hedge to your left. Enter a hedged track and follow it up to a T-junction with a Leeds Country Way signpost, where you turn right along the track. When it forks, keep right, i.e. straight on, soon passing to the left of Wike Wood. At the motor road turn right to return to the starting point.

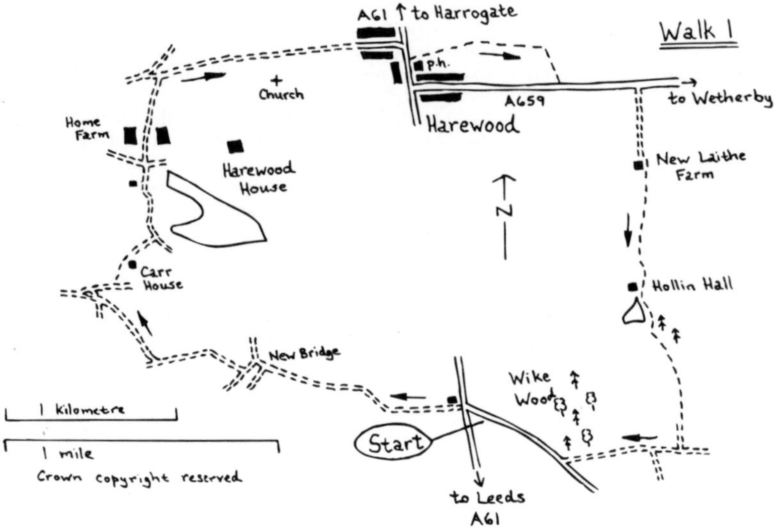

RIVER WHARFE, KEARBY, WOODHALL BRIDGE AND CARTHICK WOOD

WALK 2

7½ miles (12 km); Pathfinder 672 (SE24/34). The intention is to walk downstream from Harewood Bridge along the north bank of the Wharfe as far as the next river bridge at Woodhall, returning along the opposite bank, but the layout of the rights of way means that the walk has much more variety than a purely riverside ramble. Lovely pastoral countryside with attractive views.

By bus: No.36 Harrogate bus half-hourly from Leeds Central Bus Station. Alight at Harewood Bridge.
By car: Park in the large layby on the A61 Leeds to Harrogate road 200 yards north of Harewood Bridge (GR 313 462).

At the end of the layby nearer to the bridge, take the signposted bridleway by the post box along a track to the left of some buildings. Soon the river is closeby on the right. When you are joined by another track coming from the left, keep forward and shortly afterwards bear half-left with the track across a large field, away from the river. On approaching a hedge and a short length of wall across the line of the track, cross a little ditch and go through a small wooden gate in the wall. Keep along the lefthand edge of the next field until you meet a concrete track at a hairpin bend, where there is a wide bridge with metal side-rails. Turn left over the bridge and follow the hedged track to a right-angle bend on a tarmac road. Ignore the road to the left and keep straight on into Netherby, passing a telephone booth and a post box, and taking the first road on the right towards Kearby.

Follow the road uphill to this very attractive hamlet, ignore a No Through Road forking right on the bend, and bear sharply left with the road up Chapel Hill. At the top, just before the road junction, look left over the wall for a fine view up Wharfedale to Almscliff Crag. Then fork right along the road to Wetherby (Gill Lane). When you reach the houses at Kearby Town End the road bears left, and just round this bend there is a track forking right, passing to the left of a farm. Follow it forward to a gate with the farmyard to your right, and then keep forward with the fence/hedge to your left into a hedged track. At the end of the lane go through a gate into a field and keep with the track along the righthand edge of the field, bearing left in 100 yards with the track and hedge (ignoring the large gate on the right). Soon the track leads through a large gate into a broad fenced way. Follow this to its end (you are high up and there is a fine view over Wharfedale), cross the stile and bear left along with the fence to your left, soon bearing right with this fence to a stile in the far corner of the field. Cross this and follow the fence on your left, to pass through a gap in the facing hedge onto Paddock House Lane.

Turn right down the lane, soon following it left past Paddock House. When the road forks, keep left; there follows a long straight stretch, with the road descending gently, and at the end of it there is a righthand bend: on this bend leave the tarmac and fork left through a gate on a track, which you follow towards an old walled garden in the distance. Ignore the gate in the wall ahead at the far side of the field and turn right down the track with the walled garden to your left. Pass through two bridle-gates close together and follow the fenced path to Woodhall Bridge, the furthest point of our walk, where we cross the Wharfe. Bear right with the path, which can be muddy, but soon the path becomes a track which climbs to the A659 Harewood to Wetherby road.

The minor road to East Keswick is opposite, but we turn right for a quarter of a mile along the busy main road. This is unpleasant, because the traffic is fast and for much of the way there is no verge to walk on. At the top of a slight rise, 80 yards before a minor road forks left, take the signposted path on the right over a stile by the lefthand gate and walk down the field close to the fence on the right. There is an old hollow way, but so overgrown that it is easier to keep to the left of it. Soon a clear path bears right through the line of trees and drops straight down the slope, passes through two gateways to reach a

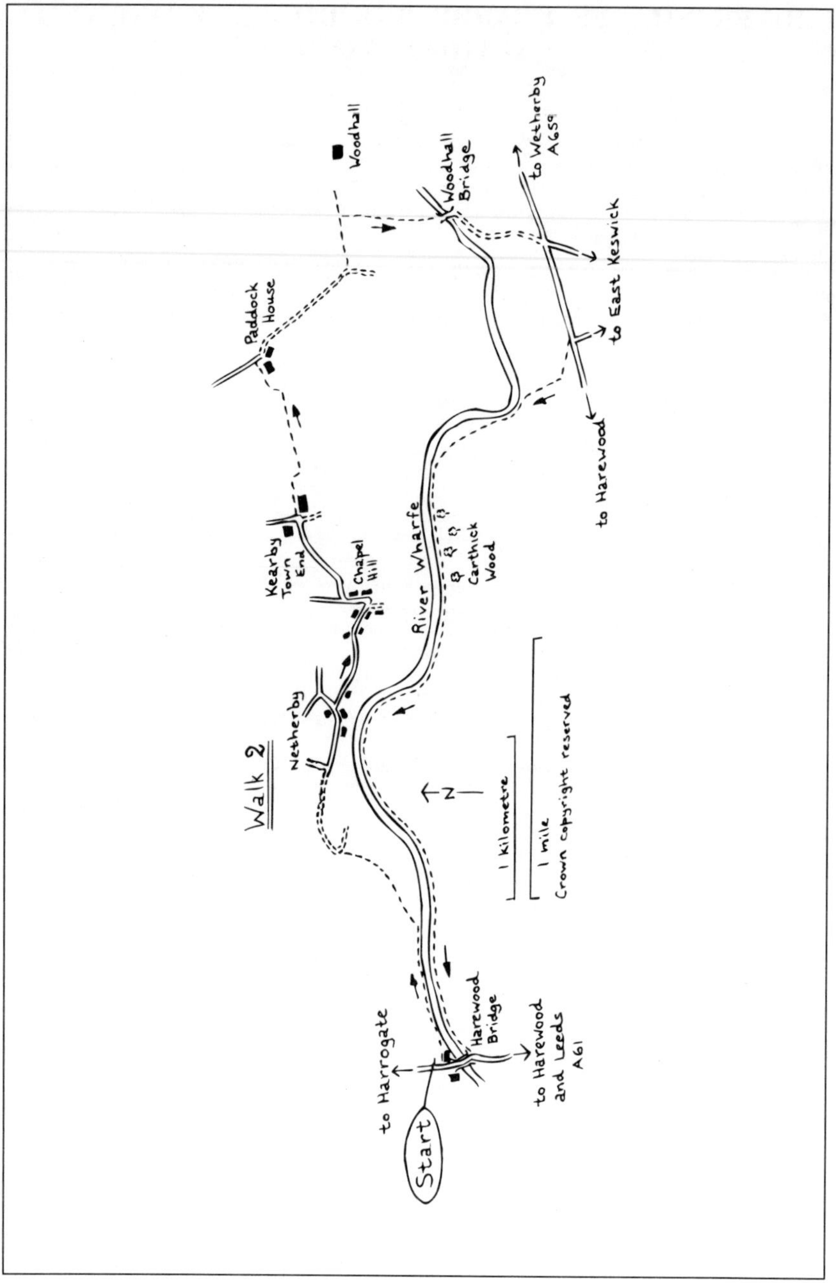
Walk 2
Start
to Harrogate
Harewood Bridge
to Harewood and Leeds A61
Netherby
Kearby Town End
Chapel Hill
River Wharfe
Carthick Wood
Paddock House
Woodhall
Woodhall Bridge
to Wetherby A659
to East Keswick
to Harewood
N
1 kilometre
1 mile
Crown copyright reserved

stile by a gate. Cross, and the river is below us. Bear left with the path downhill, bearing left again at the foot of the slope. The river is closeby on the right.

Soon bear right into a field and keep forward along the riverbank. Shortly there is a narrow wood between you and the river: do not be tempted to enter this wood, but keep along the righthand edge of the large field. And don't be diverted left at an old field boundary: keep on with the wood to your right. Soon after the wood ends you are once more close to the river. A little further and you again have a wood to the right. About 200 yards before the facing wood at the end of this field turn right on a waymarked path (be careful not to miss it) into the wood and follow the clear narrow path, which can be overgrown in summer, as it soon bears left and reaches the riverbank. Turn left along by the river. Leave the wood by a stile and continue along the righthand edge of the field.

Now essentially you follow the riverbank all the way back to Harewood Bridge, at first along the flood embankment. On the way you may pass large numbers of free range pigs, but don't worry, they are behind electric fences! After leaving the embankment follow the good track forward, but when this bears left uphill towards Harewood village, cross a stile and keep forward along the riverbank, along the righthand edge of a field. Just before an old stone building which looks like some sort of chimney the path bears right out of the field to pass to the right of this structure and proceed forward to a stile by a gate into another enormous field. Follow the righthand edge of this field, with Harewood Bridge now drawing closer, and about 100 yards before the bridge look out for a path forking half-right out of the field and descending gently closer to the river. Follow this path along to a stile out onto the main road and bear right over the bridge to return to the starting point.

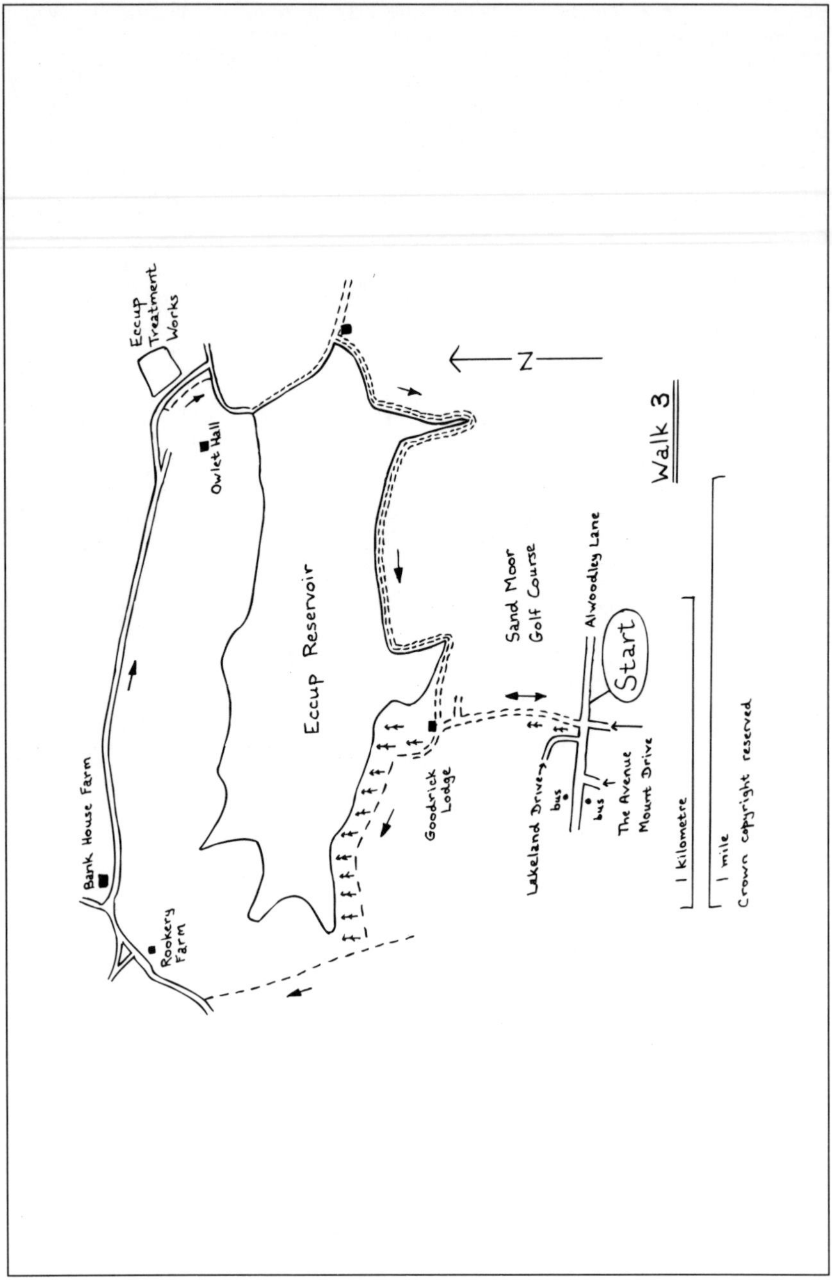

Walk 3
N
Eccup Treatment Works
Owlet Hall
Eccup Reservoir
Bank House Farm
Rookery Farm
Goodrick Lodge
Sand Moor Golf Course
Alwoodley Lane
Start
Lakeland Drive
bus
bus
The Avenue
Mount Drive
1 kilometre
1 mile
Crown copyright reserved

THE CIRCUIT OF ECCUP RESERVOIR

WALK 3

3¾ miles (6 km); Pathfinder 672 (SE 24/34). An easy pastoral stroll on clear paths, tracks and a minor/private road. The path by the reservoir is popular with joggers and twitchers!

By bus: No.34/35 from Briggate (Queen's Arcade) half-hourly. Alight on Alwoodley Lane near its junction with The Avenue, and keeping The Avenue on your right walk along Alwoodley Lane for about 200 yards until you are opposite its junction with Mount Drive.
By car: Park on Alwoodley Lane near its junction with Lakeland Drive and opposite Mount Drive.

A public footpath sign points through large white gates along a tarmac drive with a No Entry sign. Follow this drive with a small conifer wood to the left and soon Sand Moor Golf Course to the right. At the foot of the hill, with Goodrick Lodge straight ahead and the reservoir visible to the right, turn left along the track. It leads to a gate: pass through and continue with the wood to your right, soon bearing left with the fence. Follow the fence all the way to a stile on the right at the far end of the wood, and then the path leads downhill to another stile. Keep forward across the middle of the field, and towards the far side keep to the right of a hedge which you follow to another stile and a road.

Turn right along the road. In the bottom of a dip ignore another road forking left and at the top of the next rise a road coming in from the left. At the fork just before Bank House Farm keep right, pass to the right of the farm and past a No Entry sign into a Yorkshire Water private road which is also a public bridleway. Follow this as far as Eccup Treatment Works, and a few yards before a lamppost and a cattle-grid go through the signposted white gate on the right and follow the hedge on the left round. At the end of the path another white gate leads to another tarmac road, on which you must turn right. It leads over the reservoir dam. At the far side, just before the lodge, go through the kissing-gate on the right into a fenced track. Follow this all the way back to Goodrick Lodge and return up the tarmac road by your outward route to the starting point.

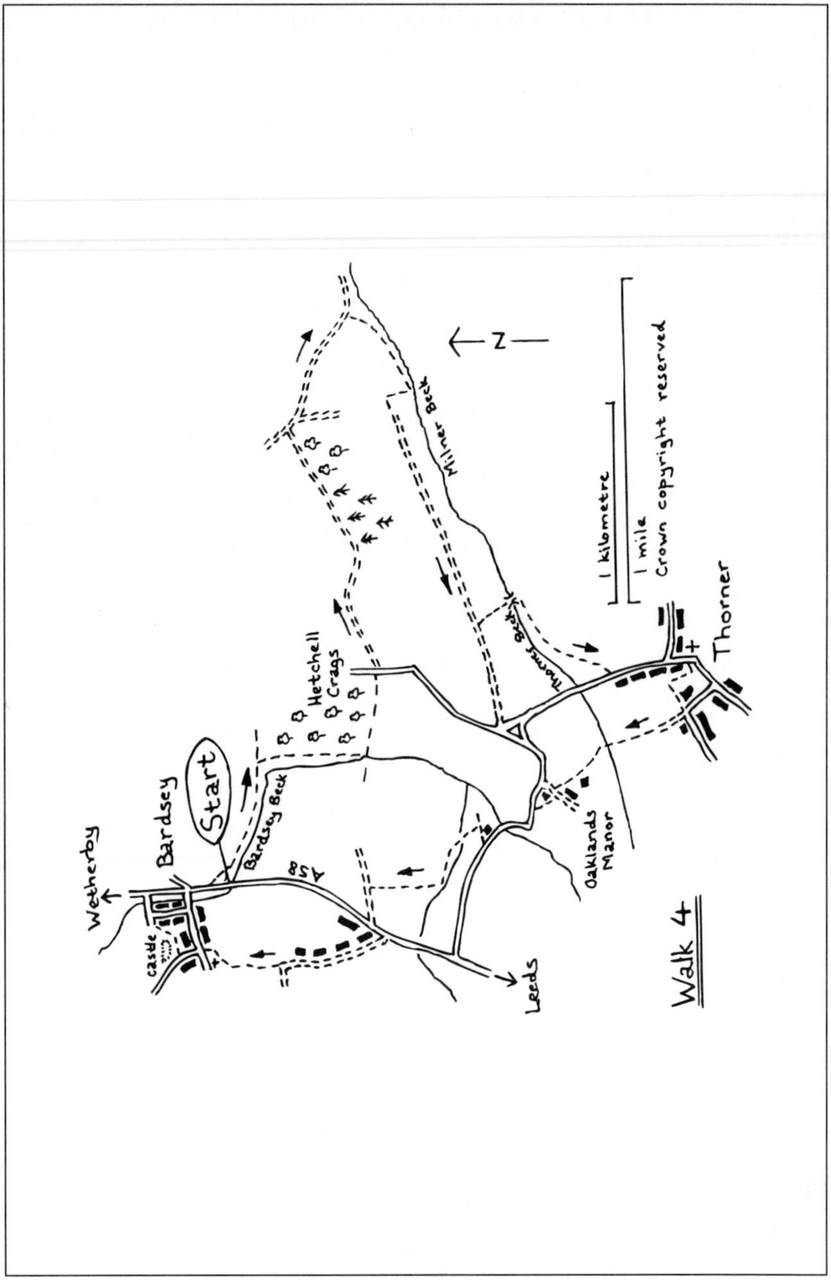
Walk 4
Wetherby
Bardsey
castle
Start
Bardsey Beck
A58
Leeds
Hetchell Crags
Oaklands Manor
Milner Beck
Thorner Beck
Thorner
N
1 kilometre
1 mile
Crown copyright reserved

BARDSEY, HETCHELL CRAGS AND THORNER

WALK 4

7 miles (11 km); Pathfinder 672 (SE24/34). A mix of woodland, arable and pasture, mainly on clear and easy paths. Part of the route is popular with horse-riders and can be muddy. The Hetchell Wood Nature Reserve merits a leisurely exploration: the route chosen here uses one of several possible paths.

By bus: No. 98, 99 Wetherby bus from Leeds Infirmary Street (half-hourly). Alight a few yards before the start of the 40 m.p.h. limit at Bardsey and walk back towards Leeds until you reach a large layby on the other side of the road.
By car: From Scarcroft the A58 Leeds to Wetherby road swings downhill to Bardsey. At the bottom of the hill, with a wood on the right, there is a large layby. Park here (GR 369 430).

Enter the wood through the bollards. The path soon joins the old railway track: bear right along it for a few yards, then fork left over a stile. The path soon follows the left hand edge of a grassy area with trees to the left, and where this ends keep forward along a clear path with a fence to your left and a hedge to your right. When the hedge bears right follow it, ignoring a clear path forward up the middle of the field. The hedge soon ends, and you keep along the bottom edge of the field with Bardsey Beck to your right. A stile leads into the woods and a noticeboard explains what is to be seen in this nature reserve (Hetchell Wood).

From the noticeboard the path bears right and climbs gently through the wood, soon passing to the right of Hetchell Crags (ignore paths forking left here). When you reach stepping stones over the beck on your right, turn left, at first with a fence to your right, but soon passing through a kissing-gate onto a track. This track, an old Roman road, is a popular bridleway and can be muddy. The earthworks over the fence on the right are known as Pompocali. Follow the track up to a motor road, then cross diagonally left to a path on the right to a large gate. Pass round the gate and continue along the edge of the field with the remains of a hedge to your right. After a time the path enters woodland, keeping close to the left hand edge of the wood. Follow it to a signposted T-junction at the far end of the wood and turn right, in a few yards keeping left at a fork.

After a time the track descends gently and you reach another fork: the left branch is about to curve left, we bear right along a narrower path. In the valley to the left is Milner Beck. Eventually you bear right at a fork and the path leads out of the woodland and along the bottom edge of a field, but after a few yards it turns right with the field edge up the slope. At the top the path turns left again, soon joining a broad track. Pass a barn and follow the track for about 1100 yards until you come to a wide gap in the hedge on the left. (Finding this gap may be tricky: it is not the first wide gap you come to, but the second, and when you turn left through it, the hedge you are going to follow down leads slightly to the left of the righthand end of the wood on the other side of the valley, a wood which has fields to the right of it.) So turn through the gap and follow the clear path down with the hedge to your right. At the bottom of the field continue downhill through the wood to cross Thorner Beck by the Jubilee Bridge.

Bear right to a stile into a field and walk straight forward across the field, soon picking up a hedge to your right. Where the hedge ends keep forward to a stile, and now again there is a hedge/fence to your right. When the hedge kinks right and then left, keep forward to cut the corner of the field to a stile which leads down some steps onto a road. Turn left along the road into Thorner. When you reach a main road bear right towards the church. Directly opposite the church tower turn right down a ginnel, which soon bears right, crosses Mill Beck, then turns left under the old railway track. On reaching a tarmac road keep forward along it, and at the main motor road continue for a few yards further, then just before the pavement starts turn right up a track.

At the end of the track cross the stile ahead and follow the hollow way with the hedge to your right. Cross another stile and keep on by the hedge, and where it ends keep forward down the right hand edge of the field to a footbridge and stile at the bottom. Now the path bears very slightly left up the next long field to a stile in the fence on the left to the right of Oaklands Manor. Continue up the walled lane, and at the end go left along the tarmac lane. Immediately after a large barn on the right go through a small metal gate on the right and walk across the lefthand end of the concrete yard to two more small gates at the far end. Once in the field walk forward to the end of the buildings on the right, then bear half-right down the field to a double stile at the next road.

Turn left down the road. Cross Scarcroft Beck, and immediately after a large white house on the right turn right along a track signposted Scarcroft and Nature Reserve. Just after the second house cross the signposted stile on the left and follow the right hand edge of the field. The well-used path soon bears right to a stile, crosses a footbridge and in a few yards reaches a field where it bears left then left again along an old hedged lane. (Be careful not to keep along the field-edge at this point.) Follow the path until it leads into a field, then keep up the right hand edge of the field. Follow the hedge on the right to a cross-track and turn left along it, ignoring the track straight ahead and keeping an old wall to your right. Now we shall complete our round with a stroll to Bardsey Church and the site of the castle. (Bus passengers who wish to end the walk here can catch a bus back to Leeds from a stop a few yards to the left along the A58.)

When you reach the A58 cross it and go left for a few yards, there turning right into Wayside Mount, an unsurfaced no through road. After the houses end pass through the gate and keep forward on the track between fields, but where the track turns sharp left keep forward and, ignoring a stile, walk down the left hand edge of the field towards Bardsey. Towards the bottom of the field the path bears half-right to cut the corner. Enter the wood, cross Gill Beck and walk up to enter the churchyard by a gate. The fine mediaeval church with its Saxon tower is worth a visit. Bear right round the east end of the church and leave the churchyard by another gate.

Walk straight forward along Woodacre Lane, the road signposted to East Keswick. Opposite Bardsey Village Hall and just past a house called Callister Hall go through a small white gate on the right and walk along the clear path with the wall of Castle Hill Nursing Home to your right and the site of the castle on the left. Pass through a gateway into a field and bear left, keeping a fence to your left, to leave the field through another gateway. Walk forward to join a cobbled drive and bear right down it. When you reach a tarmac road bear right along it, ignoring Cornmill Close and later another road on the left. Now Bardsey Beck is on your left and you reach a T-junction. This is Church Lane. Turn left to the A58. Bus passengers will cross the main road and go left for a few yards to the bus-stop. Motorists will cross the main road, ignore Wood Lane bearing left uphill, and take the path bearing right up into the wood. Soon you join the old railway track and bear left away from the main road below you. At the next path junction bear sharply right to return to the starting point

ROUNDHAY PARK, SHADWELL AND SCARCROFT

WALK 5

$7\frac{1}{2}$ miles (12 km); Pathfinder 683, 672 (SE 23/33, 24/34); a varied ramble, mainly by field and woodland paths, through undulating pastoral countryside. Roundhay Park itself, including the Canal Gardens and Coronation House with its tropical wildlife, is worth exploring at leisure, but in view of the length of today's walk, that must probably be left for another occasion.

By bus: No. 10, 12 from Marks & Spencer's in Briggate to Roundhay Park (Prince's Avenue) and walk into the old tram terminus which is now a large car park.
By car: Park at the old tram terminus (the posts which used to carry the overhead wires still survive), now a large car park, off Prince's Avenue at Roundhay Park.

From the far end of the car park follow the broad track which soon descends by a flight of steps. At the foot cross straight over the tarmac road and walk along in front of the tiers of seats, curving right towards the pavilion, but before you reach it, turn left up one of the sets of steps between the seats and cross the grass to another tarmac road coming down from the mansion up on the left. Cross it and continue forward to the brow of the hill (up to the left is the bandstand), heading towards what look like two narrow white gateposts. These turn out to mark a speed hump in another tarmac road. Again cross straight over and keep forward across the grass, soon beginning to drop towards the valley and the Waterloo Lake (it was made in 1815). As you descend, bear left towards the lefthand end of the lake and walk round it on a clear path. Up to the left is a mock mediaeval castle gatehouse.

Having crossed a sleeper bridge, don't bear right with the main lakeside path, but fork left into the woods. Keep to the valley bottom path, which leads through the lovely Roundhay Gorge. After a time the path crosses and re-crosses the beck by a series of bridges. When the path forks, keep right on the lower path up the valley bottom, with more bridges to cross. Soon the noise of traffic on the Ring Road is prominent on the right. Shortly before you reach a tall well-built stone bridge spanning the beck, go through the gap in the wall on the right and follow the path uphill to the Ring Road.

Cross with great care and go left for a few yards to the signposted footpath opposite. This leads to Shadwell. When you reach Main Street, turn right for a few yards, then cross and go left into Holywell Lane. Where the road turns sharp left go through the gateway on the right and along the stony track signposted as a public bridleway. It passes Brandon House and various other houses before reaching a junction. Here you have a choice of routes:

The **first** is more pleasant but slightly less easy to follow. Go through the gateway ahead signposted Barn Cottage Boarding Kennels and immediately turn right down the wallside to a stile in the bottom corner. Cross this and the track and the stile by the gate opposite and walk forward the few yards to the next stile. Now bear slightly left away from the fence on your right across the large field to a gate at the far end. Cross the stile by the gate and keep forward on the same line up the slope of the next field. Soon you will see that you are making for a large white gate. When you reach it, don't go through, but head back across the field at an angle of 90 degrees to the path you have just been following to a stile which is visible as a gap in the far hedge between two large trees. There is no clear path through these fields. Cross the stile and bear slightly left to walk at right angles to the hedge you have just crossed over the next field. As you come over the crest you will see that you are heading for a gateway in the next facing hedge. Pass through and keep forward by the hedge/wall on your left to Low Brandon Farm. Go through the gate into the farmyard and walk straight through it and up the access road to a minor road. Turn left for about 75 yards and keep a lookout for a signpost and stile on the right.

The **second** alternative is easy to follow, but can be excessively muddy due to heavy usage by horses and involves more road-walking. Fork left before the gateway down a

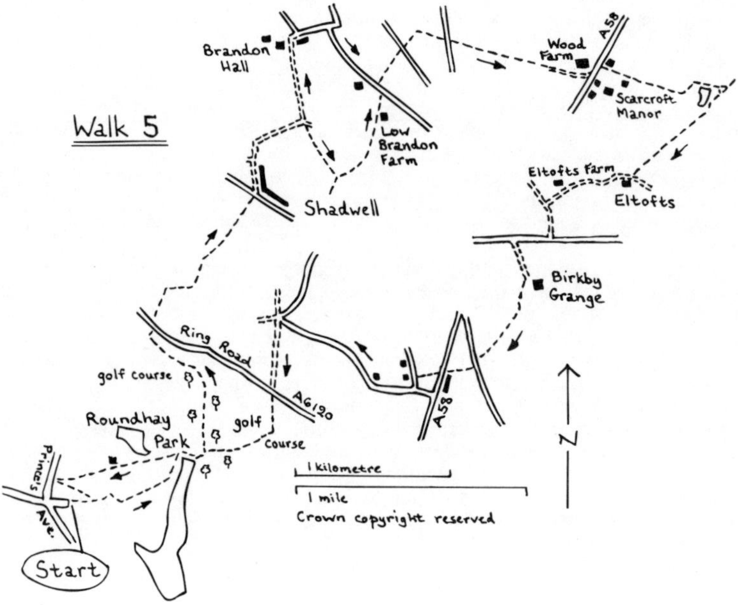
Walk 5
Brandon Hall
Low Brandon Farm
Shadwell
Wood Farm
A58
Scarcroft Manor
Eltofts Farm
Eltofts
Birkby Grange
Ring Road
A6120
A58
golf course
Roundhay Park
golf course
Prince's Ave.
Start
1 kilometre
1 mile
Crown copyright reserved
N

narrower fenced path and follow it to the T-junction at Brandon Hall Farm, where you bear right to reach a minor road. Keep straight forward along this and turn sharp right at the next junction. At the end of a stretch of wall on the left with a hedge growing on top of it you will reach a signposted footpath on the left.

The path leads through a young plantation, keeping close to the hedge/fence on the left, and over a stile into a fenced path through the nursery to another stile and the next motor road. Cross straight over to the stile opposite, just to the left of the entrance to White Hall. Follow the fence/hedge on your right, and where it bears right keep with it (it is now a wall) to a stile in the corner. The path leads to a track which you follow down to the next road. Again cross straight over to another stile, then follow the wall/fence/hedge on your left. Pass through the gateway in the far corner (or cross the stile) and continue forward across the next field. A hedge comes down from the left and again you have a fence to your left. After passing through another gateway you have a hedge to your left, and after the next gateway you are on a fenced track which you follow to the A58 Leeds to Wetherby road at Wood Farm.

Cross with care and turn left along the pavement for 60 yards to a footpath on the right signposted to Thorner. Walk up the drive towards Scarcroft Manor, but leave it just before the next gateway and pass to the left of the lodge along a narrow path initially between high walls. Cross a stile into parkland and follow the fence on your left down until shortly after reaching a wood on the left you come to a stile into it. Walk along the track to a junction with a gate ahead and the track bearing left through an old gateway, and cross the stile on the right to continue down a track through the wood. Cross the bridge by the sluice at the lefthand end of the lake and in a few yards fork right on a track which rises to the top edge of the wood. The lake is down to your right.

The clear path keeps forward some way above the lake, then continues through the wood until it leaves this through a small gate. Keep straight forward across the next field, heading for a cluster of houses in the distance. Leave the field by a stile just below the houses (Eltofts) and bear right along the lane, soon joining the access drive to Eltofts House (which is behind you). Shortly after passing Eltofts Farm the road turns left. At the motor road turn right, then after 250 yards turn left into the access road to Birkby. As the road bears left towards the buildings fork right off it and follow the hedge on the right up to a stile by a gate. Keep along with the hedge to your right. Near the far corner of the field ignore a gate on the right and go through the gate straight ahead, then bear slightly right to a gate in the next hedge just to the right of a power line pole.

Go through the gate and bear diagonally left across the next large field to a yellow marker post in the far hedge. When you reach it, keep forward with the hedge to your left to the road. Cross it and go left for a short distance to a signposted footpath opposite. Follow the hedge on the left to the next road, the A58 again. Cross to the stile opposite and walk straight over the next field to a stile by a gate just to the left of a large house. Turn left along the road, then go right at the T-junction.

When you reach thc 30 m.p.h. limit on the edge of Shadwell the road makes a sharp turn right. On this bend you must ignore the track ahead, turn left, then immediately fork left again on a track across the field. It leads once more to the Leeds Ring Road. Cross with care to the stile opposite. Walk straight forward over the golf course, heeding the notice to beware of flying balls. You reach some trees, and immediately after crossing a tiny beck fork right off the track down a couple of steps onto a clear path across more of the golf course towards the woods. Cross straight over a clear cross path and enter the wood, at first with an old wall to your left. Pass through a gap in a facing wall, cross another cross path and continue downhill through woodland. On the way you go up and then down a few steps.

Rejoin your outward route and bear left to the lake, there turning right over the sleeper bridge. Having rounded the end of the lake bear right up the slope with a wood to your right and you will reach the upper lake. Bear left to the bandstand we saw earlier, cross straight over the road and take the tarmac drive opposite, passing to the left of the mansion, built in 1826 and called by Pevsner 'the grandest of the Late Georgian mansions of Leeds'. This broad drive leads to the main gates of the Park and the bus stop. For the car park bear left shortly before reaching the Park gates.

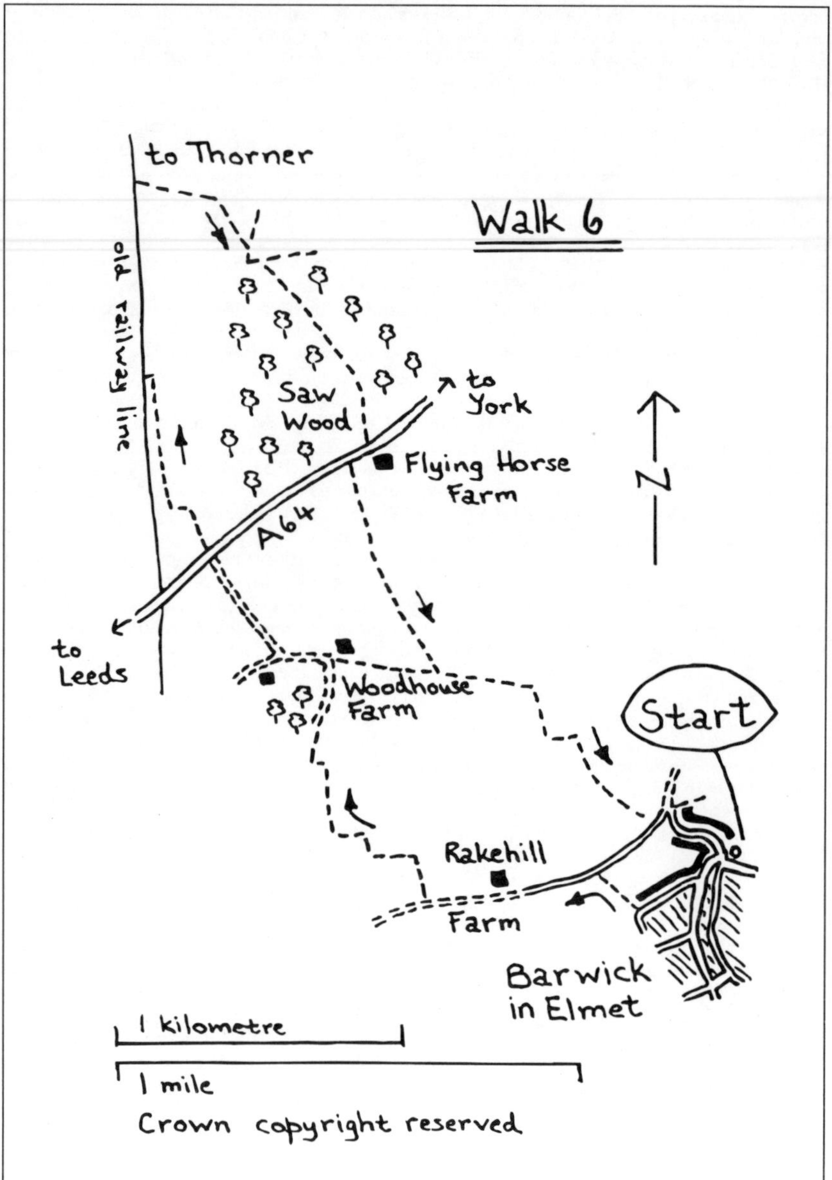
to Thorner
Walk 6
old railway line
Saw Wood
to York
Flying Horse Farm
N
A64
to Leeds
Woodhouse Farm
Start
Rakehill Farm
Barwick in Elmet
1 kilometre
1 mile
Crown copyright reserved

BARWICK IN ELMET AND SAW WOOD

WALK 6

5 miles (8 km); Pathfinder Map 683 (SE 23/33). Arable, pastoral and woodland.

By bus: *No. 64 Aberford bus from Leeds City Square (half-hourly).*
By car: *There is limited parking in Barwick Main Street, or park in Elmwood Lane, which is parallel to Main Street but west of it.*

The walk starts at the maypole in the centre of Barwick in Elmet. From the maypole walk past the side of the Gascoigne Arms along a street called The Boyle. Almost at once there is a junction: leave The Boyle, which forks right, and keep straight on along Elmwood Lane, which soon bends left. Turn right into Elmwood Avenue; between houses 30 and 32 on the right take the tarmac ginnel which soon turns right, and when the garden wall ends keep straight forward down the lefthand edge of the field. Cross a stile onto a tarmac road and turn left along it. After the tarmac ends at Rakehill Farm keep forward along the track for about 300 yards, then follow the footpath sign pointing right into a field. Walk along the edge of the field with a hedge to your left. Cross the stile in the top corner and turn sharp left. Where the hedge on your left turns sharp left again the footpath bears right across the middle of the field. After 50 yards pass a signpost and keep forward towards the wood in the distance. The houses of Scholes are off to your left. Eventually the path bears left and then by an old field corner right again, now a broad track, which passes to the right of the wood.

Follow the track to Woodhouse Farm and there turn left along the farm access track. At a fork just before Whinmoor Nook Farm bear right to the A64 Leeds to York road. Cross straight over this busy road, then the ditch by a plank bridge by the signpost and walk forward along the lefthand edge of the field. Follow the high wire fence when it turns left, and at the next field corner turn right, with the track of the old Leeds to Wetherby railway line to your left. In a few yards ignore a stone bridge over the railway and keep forward along the lefthand edge of the field. About 80 yards before a tall metal pylon take a broad track left which crosses the railway line, but turn right off it along the old bed of the railway. Cross two stiles.

About 100 yards before a double gate across the railway track with a tree to the left of it and a stile to the left of the tree, cross a stile by a gate on the right into a fenced path leading uphill under power lines. The houses of Thorner are off to your left. When the hedge on the left ends keep forward on the path, which leads to the left of another hedge ahead. Follow this hedge to the far corner of the field and turn right over the stile by the gate.

Walk along the hedged lane to the corner of the wood. Immediately after entering the wood fork half-left (yellow waymark) on a clear path through the wood. Follow this clear path forward through Saw Wood, ignoring cross paths, and reassured from time to time by marker posts with yellow arrows. At one point fairly early on in the wood there is a fork where you must keep right (a yellow arrow a few yards along confirms this). You reach the A64 again opposite Flying Horse Farm. Turn right along the road for about 50 yards then cross it with great care to a signposted path opposite. Cross the stile and walk forward with the hedge/fence to your left. When the fence turns left keep forward down the field boundary with a hedge to your left.

Cross the stile at the bottom and follow the very clear path forward across the next field. Woodhouse Farm is up to your right. At a signposted path junction bear left, soon passing through a gap in the hedge ahead and following the hedge on your right. When the hedge ends keep forward with a ditch to your right. Immediately before a large hawthorn on the right, where the hedge begins again, fork half-right across the ditch to a signpost, then forward across the middle of the field to a tree 40 yards ahead, then follow the same line to a marker post. At this point, an old field corner, turn sharp left and follow the field boundary with a hedge to your right. Keep with the field edge when it turns right, cross the stile in the next field corner and keep on with the hedge to your right to another stile ahead, by a gate on the right. Now the hedge is on your left. Cross another stile and a footbridge and walk forward for a few yards before bearing slightly left to a signpost in the top lefthand corner of the field. Turn left along the road and at the next junction bear right with it uphill back into Barwick.

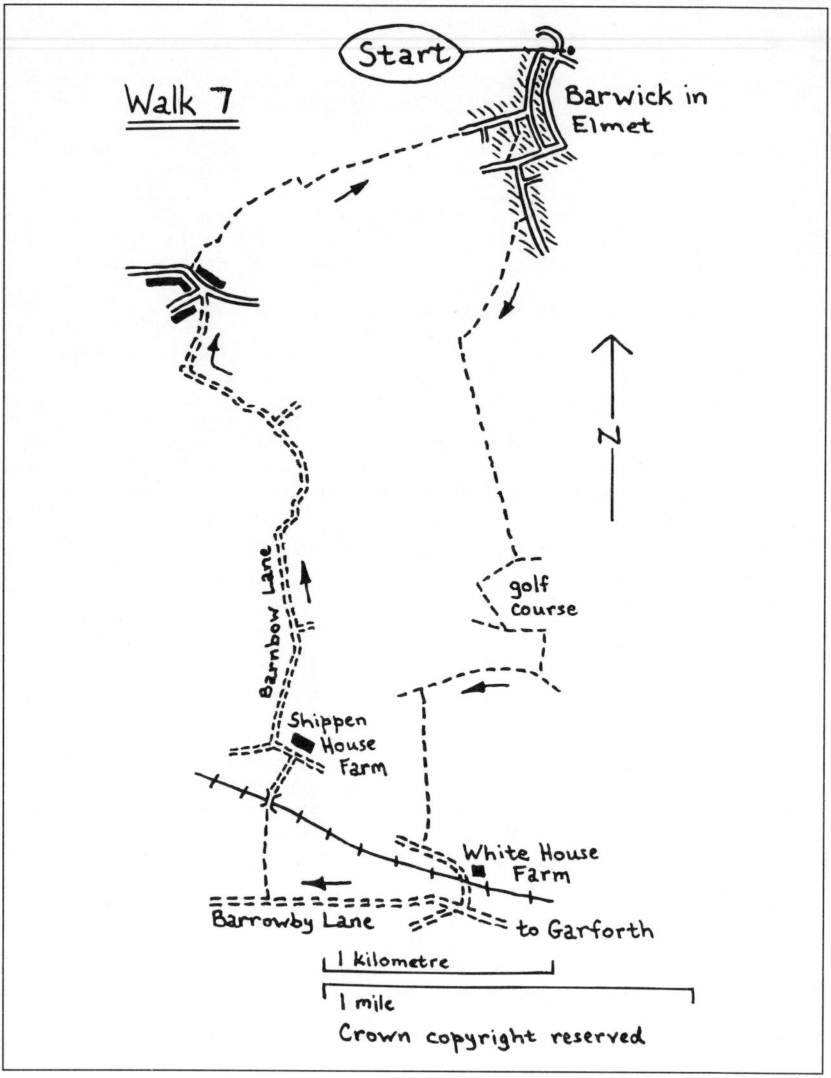

BARWICK IN ELMET AND GARFORTH CIRCULAR VIA BARNBOW LANE

WALK 7

6½ miles (10 km). Pathfinder 683 (SE23/33). Gently undulating countryside east of Leeds, including part of the Leeds Country Way.

By bus: No. 64 Aberford bus from Leeds City Square (half-hourly).
By car: There is limited parking in Barwick Main Street, or park in Elmwood Lane, which is parallel to Main Street but west of it.

The walk starts at the maypole in the centre of Barwick in Elmet. From the maypole walk past the side of the Gascoigne Arms along a street called The Boyle. Almost at once there is a junction: leave The Boyle, which forks right, and keep straight on along Elmwood Lane, which soon bends left. At a crossroads turn right into Carrfield Road. Ignore the garage access lane on the left and after 100 yards turn left into the first street, (Carrfield Road 44-64) which soon ends at a turning space, but straight ahead there is a fenced ginnel, which leads to a main road. Turn left for a few yards, then right into Flats Lane. Between numbers 32 and 34 turn right into a fenced ginnel leading to a stile. Bear half left across the narrowish field to the next stile.

Now some care is needed with route finding, although the path should be visible on the ground. From the stile walk straight forward for a few yards to cross a beck. At the far side of the field you will see a fence: you are making for a stile near the lefthand end of this fence. So bear half left towards the line of an old hedge, then follow it to the stile. Cross this and walk straight forward to the lefthand end of the hedge ahead. Bear right up the slope with the hedge to your left. Follow the edge of this field to the top corner, then turn left through the hedge, and continue with the hedge now on your right.

Crossing the rise, Garforth can be seen ahead. Follow the hedge down, crossing two stiles, to reach a third stile into a wood (FP sign pointing left to Barwick Road and Parlington, back to Barwick and right to Manor Farm and Garforth). Follow the righthand path, which leads between Garforth golf course on the left and a tall hedge on the right. Route finding on the next stretch, until you leave the golf course again, is made easier by tall wooden marker posts with yellow tops, which indicate the right of way. As you cross several fairways, there is some danger from flying golf balls. The path bears left through the wood to the edge of the golf course, then straight forward to cross a footbridge. Keep straight on up the slight slope with a hedge to your left, and just before the field corner a marker post points you through the hedge on the left. Bear slightly left over the fairway to the next marker post on the edge of a wood, and walk through the wood to the next post on the far side, then keep forward across the next fairway to a cluster of low trees with a white marker post on the nearside edge. Now bear slightly left through the trees to the next tall post, crossing a gravel path on the way, and at this post bear left along a track, which is a bridleway between Barnbow Lane and Garforth, passing a row of young conifers on your right, to the next post, which is just before the track enters trees.

Turn right and walk to the next post on the far side of a wide sleeper bridge. Now turn left and follow Cock Beck on your left. At a corner of the golf course keep forward along a track into trees, still by the beck, to the next post. Now turn right and follow the boundary fence/hedge of the golf course up to a large old footpath sign. Ignore the stile on the left and turn right along the top edge of the wood. Pass along the lefthand edge of the 4th tee and at the far side bear left to follow a hedge on your left along through trees. In about 25 yards bear left along a broad path, soon forking left up to the 6th tee. Again keep along the lefthand edge. As you walk on along the top edge of the golf course look out for a marker post on the left which points you along a path between the hedge on the left and a narrow strip of trees on the right.

Follow the hedge until you leave the woodland (and the golf course, there is a warning notice-board), and walk on along the edge of the field, keeping the hedge on your left. In 50 yards the hedge ends: here turn left and head for a wooden pylon bearing power lines. About 50 yards before you reach it cross a stile ahead and continue forward with the fence to your left to a stile in the next field corner. Cross this and follow the fence/hedge on your left over three more stiles until you climb a few yards to reach a track. Turn left along it. Enter the yard of White House Farm and bear right to cross the main Leeds-York railway (CARE!). Follow the lane to its end.

Here you join the Leeds Country Way. Turn right, taking the righthand of the two lanes which present themselves (Barrowby Lane) (Garforth is along the road to the left), and follow it until you reach a broad gateway with massive gateposts on the right with a stile beside it. Go through and follow the track with the hedge to your right. Over the rise, drop to cross the railway again and reach Shippen House Farm. Turn left along the lane, and at the next fork keep right. Soon the metalled road becomes a track (Barnbow Lane). Keep on the main track, ignoring tracks to right or left; a field's breadth before the houses at Scholes it curves sharply right; follow it to the main road. Cross this, go right the few yards to the junction, then bear left; cross this road too, and just before the road bends left, before a bus stop, turn right into a track (Leeds Country Way sign).

The track follows the hedge on the left. Where the track ends, go through a very wide gap in the hedge on the left and continue the direction as before, now on a footpath with the hedge to your right. Soon you pass under power lines. In the corner of the field cross a stile on the right and the hedge is now to your left. After 50 yards find a stile on the left, cross it and continue with the hedge to your left. In the field corner cross through a gap on the left to continue your direction now with the hedge to your right. Look out for where the path kinks through the hedge to continue on the line of an old lane towards Barwick ahead. Soon the lane is hedged, and where you reach the macadamed road keep straight on to rejoin your outward route. At the crossroads either turn left to return to the maypole or keep straight on for Main Street.

BARWICK IN ELMET TO PARLINGTON PARK

WALK 8

7½ miles (12 km); Pathfinder 683 (SE 23/33), 684 (SE 43/53). Pleasantly undulating countryside, arable, pasture and woodland; good paths.

By bus: No. 64 Aberford bus from Leeds City Square (half-hourly).
By car: There is limited parking in Barwick Main Street, or park in Elmwood Lane, which is parallel to Main Street but west of it.

The walk starts at the maypole in the centre of Barwick in Elmet. From the maypole walk past the side of the Gascoigne Arms along a street called The Boyle. Almost at once there is a junction: fork right and continue along The Boyle, a No Through Road, following it through the village and downhill. Where it forks (the lefthand branch is Rakehill Road) keep right (footpath sign to York Road) and after the tarmac ends cross Rake Beck by the footbridge and continue along the track. You are on the Leeds Country Way. At the end of the track cross the stile by the footpath sign and keep forward with a hedge to your left. Shortly after the hedge ends there is a redundant stile; keep forward and cross Potterton Beck by a footbridge.

Cross the stile on the left and walk parallel to the beck on your left. Follow the beck all the way to a stile just before the A64 Leeds to York road. Here you leave the Leeds Country Way. Don't cross this stile, but turn right with the fence/wall to your left until you reach another stile in it. Don't cross this one either, but head back across the field, aiming just to the right of the small wood, and keeping the trees on your left follow them along to a redundant stile; at this point bear slightly left and keep the remainder of the trees to your right, to reach a stile. Cross and look right to find the next stile, after which you have a fence on your right. Cross another stile and soon the fence is joined by a hedge. Cross another stile and turn right, still with the hedge to your right. In the next corner turn left again and follow the hedge to a road.

Bear right along it, ignoring the access road to the farm on the right, and at the next junction ignore Potterton Lane on the right and keep straight on. Where the road turns sharp left, with the entrance into Potterton Hall ahead, turn right along a track (Miry Lane). Follow this all the way to where it drops into a dip and reaches a T-junction. Turn right, with a deep ditch on the right. Shortly after bending slightly left the track passes through an embankment called on the map The Ridge, and at the foot of the next field it turns left. Just before a pond turn right off the main track and follow the path until you cross Cock Beck and reach a gate into a field. Bear half-left over the next field to pass through a line of trees onto a track which climbs the bank, passing well to the right of an isolated house, and just to the left of the farm buildings, to a gate in the top corner. Leaving Leyfield Farm to your right, follow the track to the Barwick to Aberford road.

Turn right for a few yards, then cross and go through the large double gate into a narrow wood. You have now entered the Parlington Estate. The route through the wood is marked by large yellow arrows painted on trees. The wood widens and the track curves left: keep left at the fork on this bend. When you reach the edge of the wood at a field corner, the track turns sharply right and climbs gently to the other edge of the wood. Here bear left and follow the path up to the right of the wood, but at the top edge of the field on your right keep straight forward through the trees to reach another large field. On the far side you will see a stile by a gate, and there should be a clear path across to it. The houses of Aberford can now be seen to your left.

From the stile bear slightly right to cross a tarmac road (look right to see the triumphal arch, erected in 1783 to commemorate 'Liberty in N.America triumphant') and descend right to a fence corner, where you bear left with the fence to your right. Follow the fence to the next stile and turn right along the track (Parlington Lane). When you reach a fork keep right on the main track to pass through a tunnel. Pass to the right of Keeper's Cottage, ignoring the entrance gates on the right. At the next houses, the Old Coal Staith, ignore a track forking left. Ignore an access road on the right to Throstle Nest Farm, cross Cock Beck and follow the track to the Barwick to Garforth road.

Immediately opposite is the access road to Willow Park Farm: follow this for 80 yards to a footpath sign pointing right through the hedge onto Garforth Golf Club's course. The right of way across the golf course is marked by tall wooden marker posts with yellow tops. So walk straight across the fairways to the next post, taking care not to be struck by flying golf balls. The post after that is just before some young trees, and to find the next one you have to continue your line through these trees. From it you can see the next post by the hedge on the far side. Bear left there, keeping the hedge to your right, passing the 18th tee and entering woodland. When you reach a large wooden signpost and a stile on the right cross this and follow the hedge/fence on your left up through several fields, Barwick appearing half-right ahead as you cross the rise.

Where the remains of the hedge begin to bear right cross through it (marker post) and turn right on a very clear path, now with the hedge to your right. The path descends gently and bears left to a stile. Cross this, pass to the left of a blackthorn bush, and you will see the next stile in the facing hedge. Cross and bear half-left over the next field to a stile leading into a ginnel. At the street turn left, and at the main road there is a bus stop for buses back to Leeds. To return to the maypole cross the main road and go left for a couple of yards to find a ginnel on the right. Follow this to its end, walk forward along the street to the T-junction, turn right and at the next main road go left to return to the village centre.

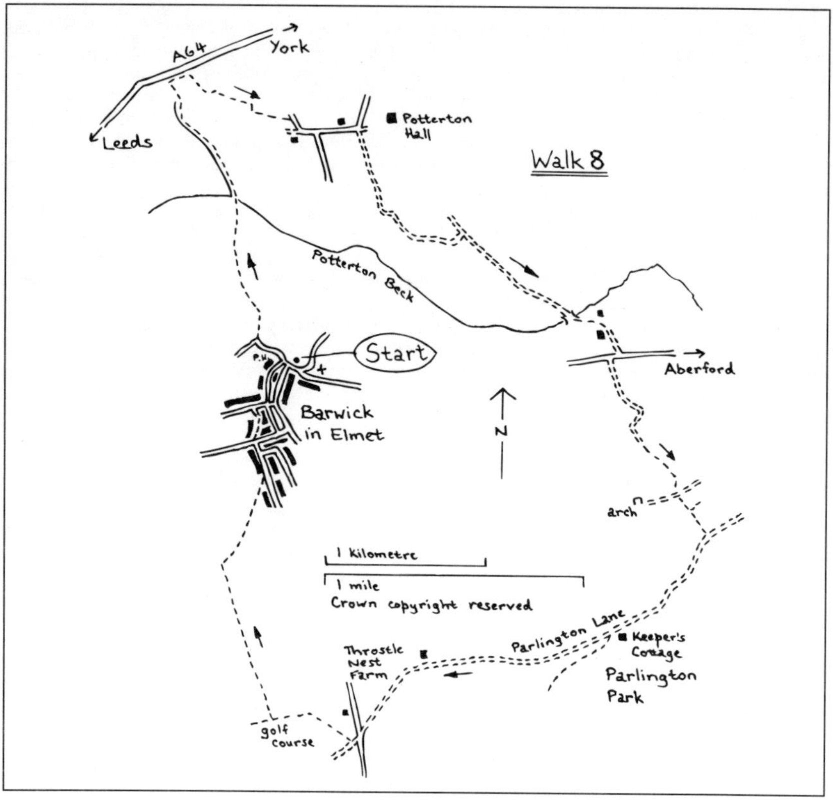

KIPPAX TO MICKLEFIELD AND LEDSHAM

WALK 9

$9\frac{1}{4}$ miles (14.7 km); Pathfinder 684 (SE43/53). An easy ramble in the limestone belt east of Leeds, woodland, pasture and parkland. The only drawback is one nasty crossing of the A1: I recommend doing this walk at the weekend, when the road can be quieter. (When the A1 is upgraded to motorway status, a safe crossing will be provided at this point.)

By bus: *No. 163, 165, 166 Castleford bus from outside the Bond Street Centre in Boar Lane, Leeds to the centre of Kippax.*
By car: *there is a car park about 50 yards below the west tower of Kippax Parish Church on the south side.*

Walk up and enter the churchyard by the west tower of the fine Norman church. Turn left before the tower and keep close to the lefthand edge of the churchyard. The path soon bears right and leaves the churchyard through a gate on the east side. Turn left along the tarmac ginnel, then right at the T-junction, still with part of the churchyard to your right. Keep forward to a road junction and continue straight on along Sandgate Terrace. Where the allotments on the left end go left along a track, and where the track curves left into the allotments and the path ahead forks, ignore the tarmac path forking right (our return route) and keep straight on.

About 50 yards after leaving the last houses of Kippax the path forks: keep right, passing to the left of a wooden pylon. The path broadens to a track which after a time swings left, becomes metalled and reaches a cross track. Turn right and follow this track to the A63. Turn right, soon crossing the road to the footway on the other side. At the roundabout cross straight over the A656 and continue along the A63 for another 400 yards until you turn left at a bridleway sign along a track. When you reach a tarmac road, cross straight over and continue along the track. Ignore a minor track forking left to Warren Farm and follow the line of overhead power lines forward. Pass round the end of a wooden fence, and now you have a wire fence on the right.

On reaching houses the path broadens to a track again and then becomes a tarmac road. At the roundabout ignore the road on the right and walk straight forward to cross the Leeds to York railway line (care!). Follow the track forward, with a football ground to the right and the houses of Micklefield over to the left. Beyond the football pitch there is a children's playground to the right of the track. Just before the track reaches a motor road fork left along a tarmac footpath which crosses a small concrete bridge and rises to Micklefield. Immediately after the school turn right and walk forward to reach the village street, the Old Great North Road, with the Blands Arms (Samuel Smith) a few yards to the right.

Cross the road and take the signposted track opposite. At the A1 the track bears left, and at the top of the slope you turn right to cross the bridge over the A1. On the far side turn right again. At the next junction keep forward, still with the A1 to your right. About 20 yards before the track crosses a beck, with filter beds beyond, fork left off it along a fairly clear narrow path, parallel to the beck over on your right and heading towards woodland. The path enters the woods and becomes a track. Follow the track, which in time narrows to a path again, until 15 yards before it leaves the top side of the wood through a gate you fork right along a clear path, which keeps fairly close to the top edge of the wood. Eventually it bears slightly right and drops to emerge from the wood with a high railway embankment to the left. Follow this forward until you turn left and pass through a tunnel under the railway.

Bear half-left with the track across the field to the next wood. A few yards after you enter the trees turn right off the track (marker post) along a clear but narrow path. Soon you must cross the railway line to Selby (care again!). Soon there is a steep drop to the right of the path and you must bear right round the edge of this, ignoring a path forking left on this bend. A short distance further on you reach another fork, where you take the left branch ahead. When you reach a clear cross path turn right along it. A few yards before you reach the A1 again the main path bears left through bollards, but you fork right up to the main road.

It is dual carriageway, so you can take it in two parts, climbing the crash barrier between them, but visibility is not very good to the right and the road is usually very busy. Having safely reached the other side, cross another minor road and go left for a few yards to enter the wood through a gateway just to the right of a bench. The path stays fairly close to the righthand edge of the wood. When you reach a fork, keep left, and a few yards further on left again, and you will emerge on to the A63 again. Turn right along it, as far as the start of the next wood on the lefthand side of the road; here cross the road and follow the sign pointing left along a track with the wood on your right. Where this wood ends, another sign points left over a stile. Walk along the clear grassy path through recently planted trees, with a young wood to the right. The next stile leads into Ledston Park, an enormous expanse of parkland, where the going is attractive but navigation none too easy. From the stile bear half-right up the grass, aiming for what looks in the distance like a gap between the woodland on the left and that on the right. You should soon pick up a clear narrow trod. As you breast the first rise you will see a group of three mature trees close together: the path passes between them, then bears slightly left to pass through the various groups of trees. Look left to see the well-preserved 17th-century Ledston Lodge.

Look out also for a signpost in the middle of the park, which gives you the further direction of the path: you must bear right, still down through the park, almost parallel to, but gradually approaching the wood on the left. As you come over the rise you will see that you are heading for a stile into the woods by a notice-board. Cross the stile and walk forward along a line of old fence posts. When you reach a broad track, bear left down it. At the next junction, going left would take you into the lovely village of Ledsham, with its Saxon church and refreshments in the Chequers Inn, but the walk turns sharp right (public footpath sign) along another track.

Where the track forks, keep following the edge of the wood on your right. Where this ends and the track bears right into a lower field, keep straight forward with a hedge to your right. Cross a stile in a piece of fence ahead, and once more you have a wood to your right. Soon a stile by a gate ahead takes you into a field, and now you are separated from the wood by a gallop. Keep along with the fence on your right, cross a stile in the next corner, and continue by the fence until you reach a stile in it. Cross this, then the gallop, then the next stile and in a few yards another stile, and walk forward with the wall of Sheepcote Farm to your right. Where this turns sharp right, bear very slightly right over the field (the farmhouse is to your right) to a stile in a fence corner, and continue with a fence and soon yet another wood to your right.

Cross a wooden footbridge and turn right, still following the edge of the wood. Pass through a gap in a facing hedge and continue along the righthand edge of the field with a narrow strip of woodland to the right. Follow the field edge to the A656 and turn left along the footway. In about 100 yards cross the road and take the signposted tarmac path back to Kippax. At the allotments you rejoin your outward route, which you re-trace back to your starting-point.

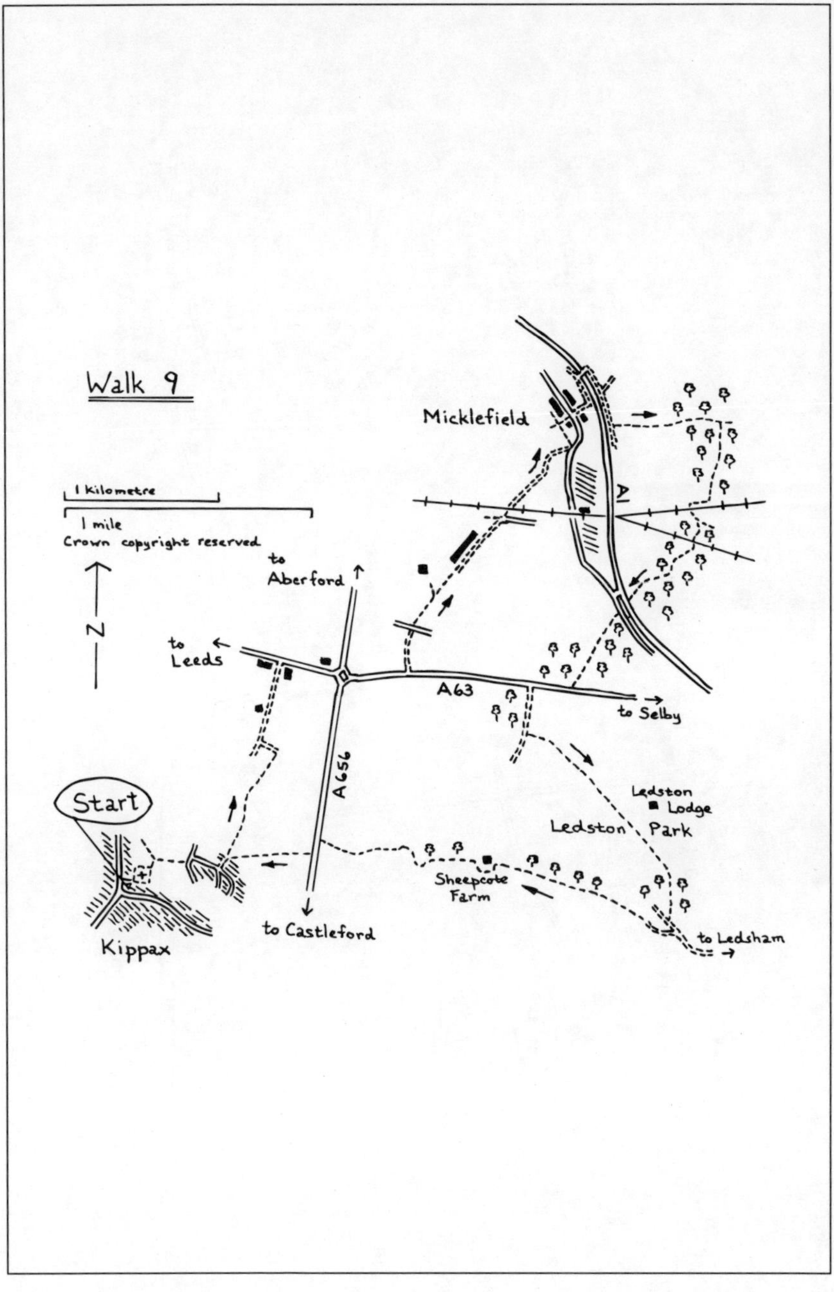
Walk 9
Micklefield
1 kilometre
1 mile
Crown copyright reserved
N
to Aberford
to Leeds
A63
to Selby
A656
Start
Ledston Lodge
Ledston Park
Sheepcote Farm
to Castleford
Kippax
to Ledsham

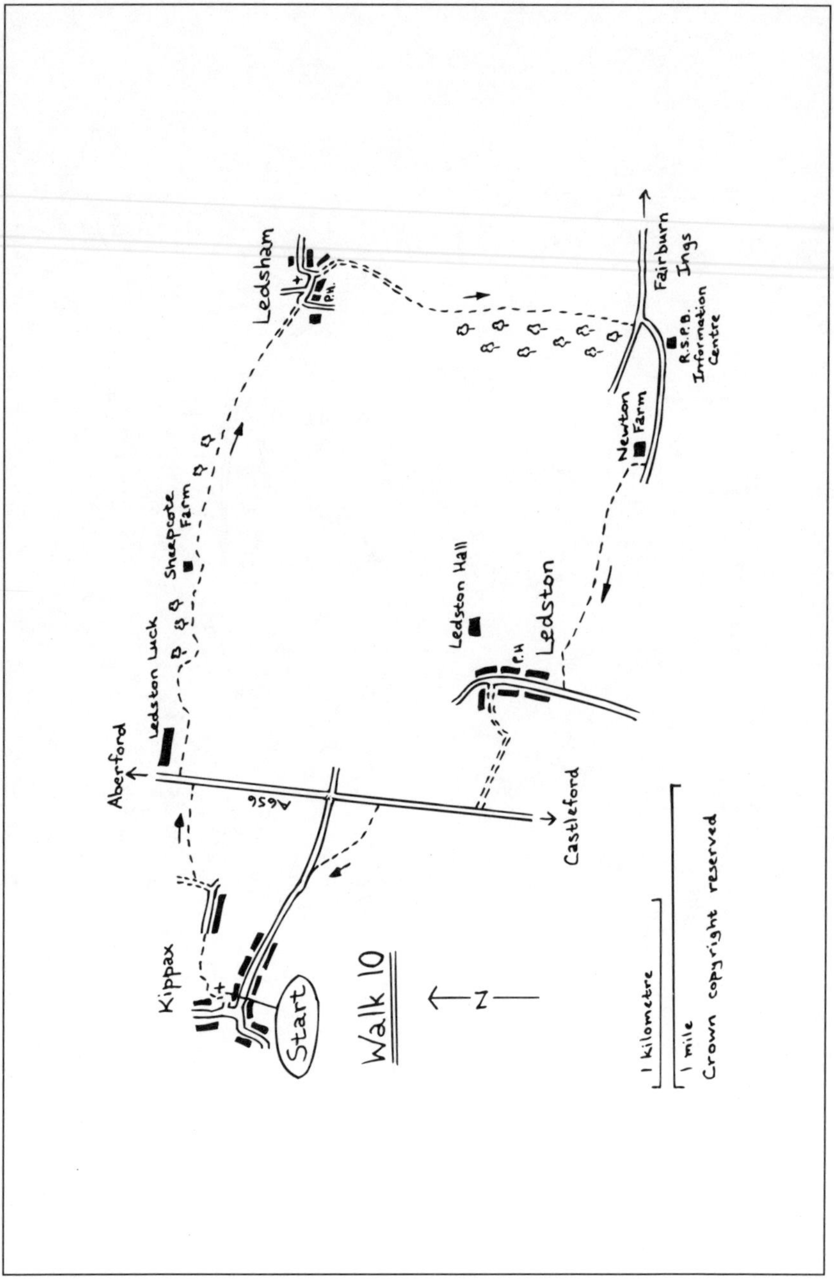

Walk 10
Start
Kippax
Aberford
A656
Castleford
Ledston Luck
Sheepcote Farm
Ledsham
P.H.
Ledston Hall
Ledston
P.H
Newton Farm
R.S.P.B. Information Centre
Fairburn Ings
N
1 kilometre
1 mile
Crown copyright reserved

KIPPAX TO LEDSHAM, FAIRBURN INGS AND LEDSTON

WALK 10

6½ miles (10 km); Pathfinder 684 (SE 43/53), 693 (SE 42/52).

By bus: No. 163, 165, 166 Castleford bus from outside the Bond Street Centre in Boar Lane, Leeds to the centre of Kippax.
By car: there is a car park about 50 yards below the west tower of Kippax Parish Church on the south side.

Walk up and enter the churchyard by the west tower of the fine Norman church. Turn left before the tower and keep close to the lefthand edge of the churchyard. The path soon bears right and leaves the churchyard through a gate on the east side. Turn left along the tarmac ginnel, then right at the T-junction, still with part of the churchyard to your right. Keep forward to a road junction and continue straight on along Sandgate Terrace. Where the allotments on the left end go left along a track, and at the next path junction keep right on the tarmac path across the fields.

When you reach the A656 Castleford to Aberford road (a very straight Roman road) cross to the footway and turn left for 100 yards to a footpath sign pointing right down into the field, near the former Ledston Luck colliery. The path follows the lefthand edge of the field. When you reach the end of a wood on the left, the path turns sharp left over a wooden footbridge, then continues along the field edge. At Sheepcote Farm there is a stile by a gate in the field corner. Bear slightly right across the field to a wall corner, and follow the wall on your left up to another stile (redundant), then forward to another stile and over the gritted gallop to another stile. Bear left round the edge of the field.

Cross the stile in the far corner of the field and continue with the fence and gallop to your left to the next stile, where the path joins the gallop. At the end of the wood cross the stile in the fence ahead and keep forward along the lefthand edge of the field (do not be tempted to cross left into the next field). Soon you have another wood to the left and the path becomes a clear track which enters woodland. You are joined by another track from the left and in a short distance you reach Ledsham. Walk straight through this lovely village, keeping the Chequers Inn on your right and the most interesting Saxon parish church on the left.

Immediately after the church, where the road bears left, turn right along a No Through Road. After 200 yards fork left onto a narrower tarmac lane which soon becomes an unsurfaced track. Shortly after you leave the village behind the track forks and you must keep right. The track narrows to a path, and Ferrybridge Power Station is prominent ahead. The path soon reaches a wood and keeps along its lefthand edge, which it follows to the next road. The large lake which appears half-left ahead is Fairburn Ings Nature Reserve.

Turn left along the road, then right at the T-junction. Just after passing a large RSPB car park on the left there is the entrance to the Fairburn Ings Information Centre, where there is also a hide. Follow the motor road past Newton Farm on the right. Just beyond it the road bends right then left: leave it on this bend to pass through the entrance to the Dandibrush Kennels on the right. In a few yards cross a stile on the right and bear left up a grassy track. At the top of the slope bear left along a clear cross track. The view left is over Newton Ings to Castleford.

Shortly after passing under the power lines carried by wooden pylons the track bears right: keep forward here along the old field boundary. Shortly after you pick up a hedge on the left, a signpost points you half-right across the field – there should be a clear path. Cross the stile on the far side and walk down the edge of the next field with the fence to your right. Cross the stile and bear right along the road through Ledston, another attractive village.

Near the far end of Ledston turn left along Green Lane (there is a view half-right up to Ledston Hall). At Ledston School the surface ends and the track leads back to the A656. Cross to the footway and turn right along the road for 500 yards to where a footpath signpost points left through the hedge. Follow the clear path over the fields to the next road, and turn left along it to return to Kippax.

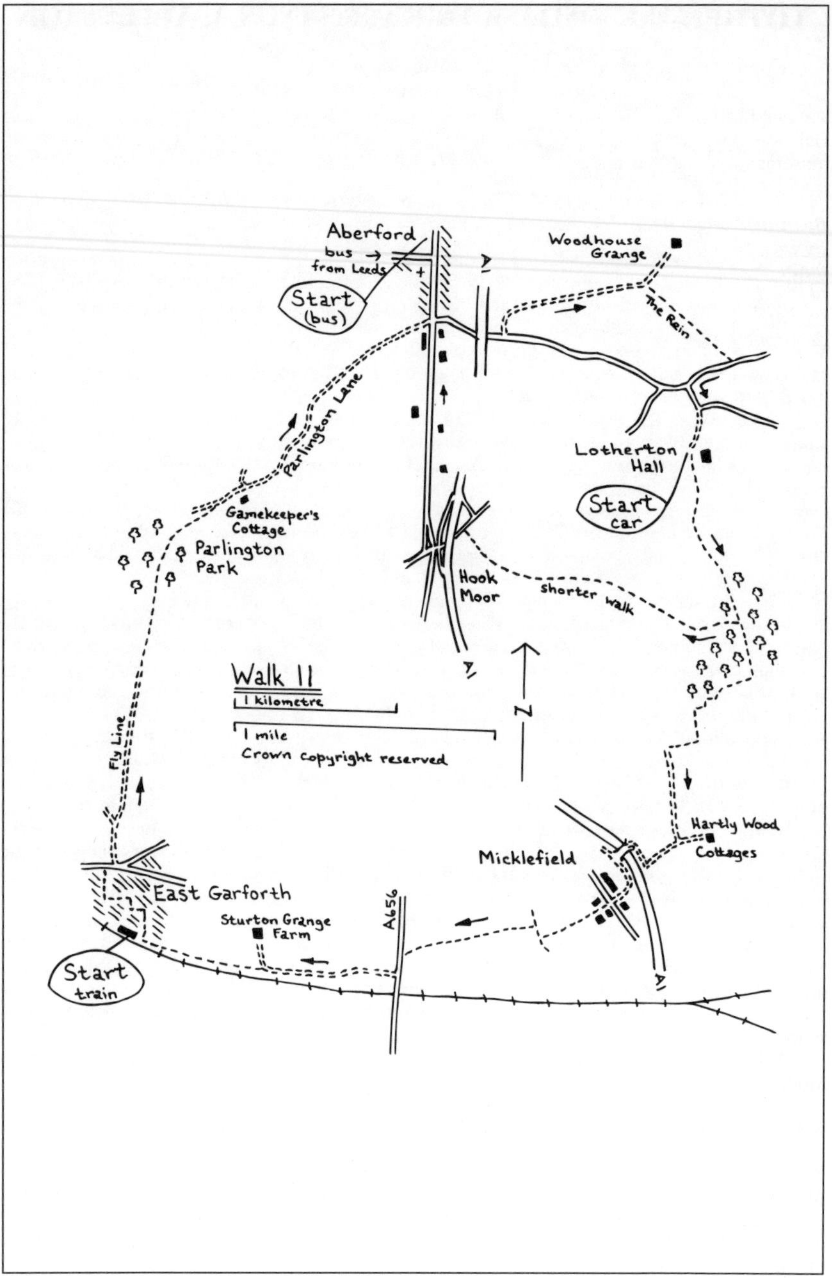
Aberford
bus from Leeds
Start (bus)
Woodhouse Grange
The Rein
Lotherton Hall
Start car
Parlington Lane
Gamekeeper's Cottage
Parlington Park
Hook Moor
Shorter walk
A1
Walk 11
1 kilometre
1 mile
Crown copyright reserved
N
Fly Line
Hartly Wood Cottages
Micklefield
East Garforth
Sturton Grange Farm
A656
Start train

LOTHERTON HALL FROM GARFORTH OR ABERFORD

WALK 11

9 miles (14½ km) or 4 miles (6 km); Pathfinder 684 (SE43/53). The Edwardian Lotherton Hall was given to Leeds by the Gascoigne family in 1968 and is now one of the Leeds art museums, specialising in oriental pottery and porcelain and in costume. The Bird Garden is popular with children. The House is closed on Mondays.

By train: (longer walk) Leeds to East Garforth Station (York & Selby Line).
By bus: (shorter walk) No. 64 from Leeds City Square to Aberford (walk south along the main street until you reach Lotherton Lane, turn left along it and join the walk description at [*] below).
By car: the most convenient starting point is Lotherton Hall (GR 449 360) (join the walk description at [#] below).

The start of the walk is dull, but after a few minutes we are out in the country. Having left the train from Leeds, don't cross the tall red footbridge, but walk past it down the slope and where the tarmac path forks keep left. Follow the path up to where it ends at a cross street, turn left for a few yards then right along Harlech Way. Turn along the first street on the left, Stirling Way, then go left at the next T-junction for a few yards to find a fenced ginnel on the right with allotments to the right of it. When you reach a tarmac path turn right along it, soon entering another unsurfaced ginnel ahead which leads to a main road (the A642). Cross over and turn right, but in a short distance turn left down Ash Lane. Where it forks keep right, then straight along the track to the right of the concrete works and so on to the old Fly Line.

Just before a brick house on the right, ignore a right and then a left fork, and when the track bears left through a gate, keep forward through a squeeze stile and along a narrower path. Cross straight over a cross track and follow the path to another squeeze stile, where you join Parlington Lane. Keep forward past the Gamekeeper's Cottage, ignoring a track bearing left through a gate, and follow the track through the longer and the shorter tunnel all the way to Aberford. Cross straight over the old A1 and along Lotherton Lane. [*] The road bears right and then left under the new A1. Take the first lane on the left, a no through road.

Follow the road to where it is crossed by a band of trees and a low mound: this is The Rein, believed to be an Iron Age boundary. Turn right off the road a few yards beyond this over a stile by a large gate and follow the track with the trees to the right. Cross a cattle-grid near a house on the right and follow the hedged track to the next motor road. Turn right along it, then left along the next minor road (signposted Sherburn in Elmet), and when this bends left, fork right off it into the grounds of Lotherton Hall, passing a large car park on the left. When you reach the buildings, either bear right to return to the car, or keep forward to [#] pass between the stable block and the Hall and continue along a paved path to pass through some trees and a kissing-gate into a paddock. Walk straight through, and leave it by another kissing-gate in the far righthand corner. A clear path leads forward through the fields. Shortly after picking up woodland on the left, the path itself enters the woods.

When you reach a clear cross track, the SHORT WALK turns right (signposted Hook Moor) and follows the track through Bragdale all the way to the main road at Hook Moor, traffic on the A1 becoming increasingly noticeable as you walk. Turn left along the road to pass under the A1, then take the second road on the right (signposted Aberford), pass one of the entrances to Parlington Park on the left and follow this Roman road, the old A1, back to Aberford (there is a footway on the left), noticing the Victorian Gothic Gascoigne Almshouses on the left on the way.

The LONG WALK crosses straight over the cross track (signpost to Micklefield) along a clear woodland path. When you reach a fork keep left, i.e. straight on, and at the far end of the wood bear right along its edge, ignoring a path straight ahead. Where the edge of the wood makes a sharp turn left, you meet a cross path; turn left with the wood, and shortly after follow it right again. In 200 yards the wood on the right ends and your path, now a broad track, turns sharp left through the fields. Just over the rise, with Hartly Wood Cottages up to the left, you meet a cross track: turn right down it towards Micklefield. Just before the A1 turn right at another T-junction and follow this track when it turns left to cross the A1 by a bridge. On the far side turn left again, and the track soon bears right to Micklefield.

Cross straight over the main street, passing to the left of the fish shop, then to the right of the school, and forward on a grassy track through the fields. When you meet a cross track turn right for 20 yards, then left off it onto a narrow path along an old field boundary, which does not seem to be much used and can be overgrown and quite hard work. Eventually you find yourself walking to the left of an old barbed-wire fence which leads to an old stile in the next field corner. Cross this and continue forward across the middle of the next field to another stile and the Roman Road (A656).

Cross the road and turn left for 100 yards, then take the access road to Sturton Grange Farm on the right. When this bears right to the farm and another track goes left over a railway bridge, keep forward over the stile by the gate and walk along the field edge with a hedge to the left. Cross another two stiles and continue forward along the road. When the road bears right. keep forward along the tarmac path to return to East Garforth Station. Motorists should fork right along a tarmac path just before reaching the footbridge over the railway and then go back to the start of the walk description.

BRAMHAM PARK AND HAZLEWOOD CASTLE

WALK 12

10½ miles (17 km); Pathfinder 673 (SE44/54), 684 (SE43/53); an easy ramble, mainly on good tracks and field paths, through the pastoral and wooded countryside of the Magnesian limestone belt east of Leeds. At present the walk involves one crossing of the busy A1, but when this is upgraded to motorway status, a bridge or underpass will be provided at this point and the route may be slightly changed: look out for waymarks.

By bus: No. 760 Wetherby bus from Leeds Central Bus Station to Bramham.
By car: Park on the old Great North Road in Bramham – there is a suitable layby just south of the village (GR 424 425).

Make your way to the main crossroads in the village centre. Have a stroll through this lovely limestone village, up to the Norman church, before returning to this point. Face the war memorial, with the Red Lion on your left, then walk half-right to take the No Through Road to the left of Bay House called Almshouse Hill. Follow it steeply up, bearing left to pass through the bollards, ignore Crag Gardens forking left, join Freely Lane and bear left along it. The large house over the high wall at the top of the slope is Bramham Lodge.

When you reach the main road cross straight over into the No Through Road opposite. After the tarmac ends keep forward along the unsurfaced track to meet another narrow motor road. Again cross straight over and walk along the drive to Headley Hall (Leeds University's farm). When the drive forks bear right, passing to the right of a long low building, towards a prominent water tower. Here fork left again, still on the concrete track. Immediately before you reach a large building set back on the right, turn right off the track and pass first to the right of this building, then bear left along behind it past the silos. At the far end turn right along a track into a field, then left along the left hand edge of this field, following a row of power lines. Pass through a gateway at the end of the field and turn sharp right along the edge of the next field, now with the fence to your right. The noisy A64 is now ahead of you. At the end of the field bear left with the field boundary, to reach the main road over a stile.

Turn right along the footway until you reach a large semi-circular tarmac area just after a bus stop, then cross the A64 with great care into a farm drive signposted to Hazlewood and Stutton. At Beck House Farm the track bears right and leads to Hazlewood Castle. With the entrance to the castle immediately ahead (it's worth taking a look inside the courtyard at the late 13th-century chapel and the Georgian rebuilding of the castle) turn sharp left and in a few yards ignore a track forking right. Turn into the next track on the right by a small barn, but only for about 50 yards, until you reach a stile on the right. Walk up the right hand edge of the field, passing a filter-bed and a small copse. Cross another stile and bear right, then left, round the field edge. There is a fine view of the castle to your right.

Follow the field edge to another stile into a small wood. Walk forward through this, passing the end of a wall and on with a fence to your right. At the far end of the wood turn left along a track, but only for about 60 yards until a marker post points half-right towards the right hand of the two small woods you will see ahead. Pass to the left of this wood and follow its edge round right to a footpath sign at the far end pointing sharp left across the field (clear path) to another signpost at a broad track, along which you turn left towards a large wood. When you reach this, leave the track and turn right along its outside edge. When you reach a point where the wood goes sharp left and a signpost points both right and back the way you have come, your path continues straight forward across the middle of the field. Soon you will see another tall signpost ahead and reach a stile by a gate in a facing fence. Cross this and keep forward with a fence to your right to pass the tall signpost and a stile to another stile ahead, beyond which you can see another signpost.

When you reach this signpost you have Cock Beck ahead of you. Turn sharp right over a stile into scrubland and follow the clear path parallel to the hedge on the right. Eventually the path bears right up the slope to another sign and stile by a gate. Keep

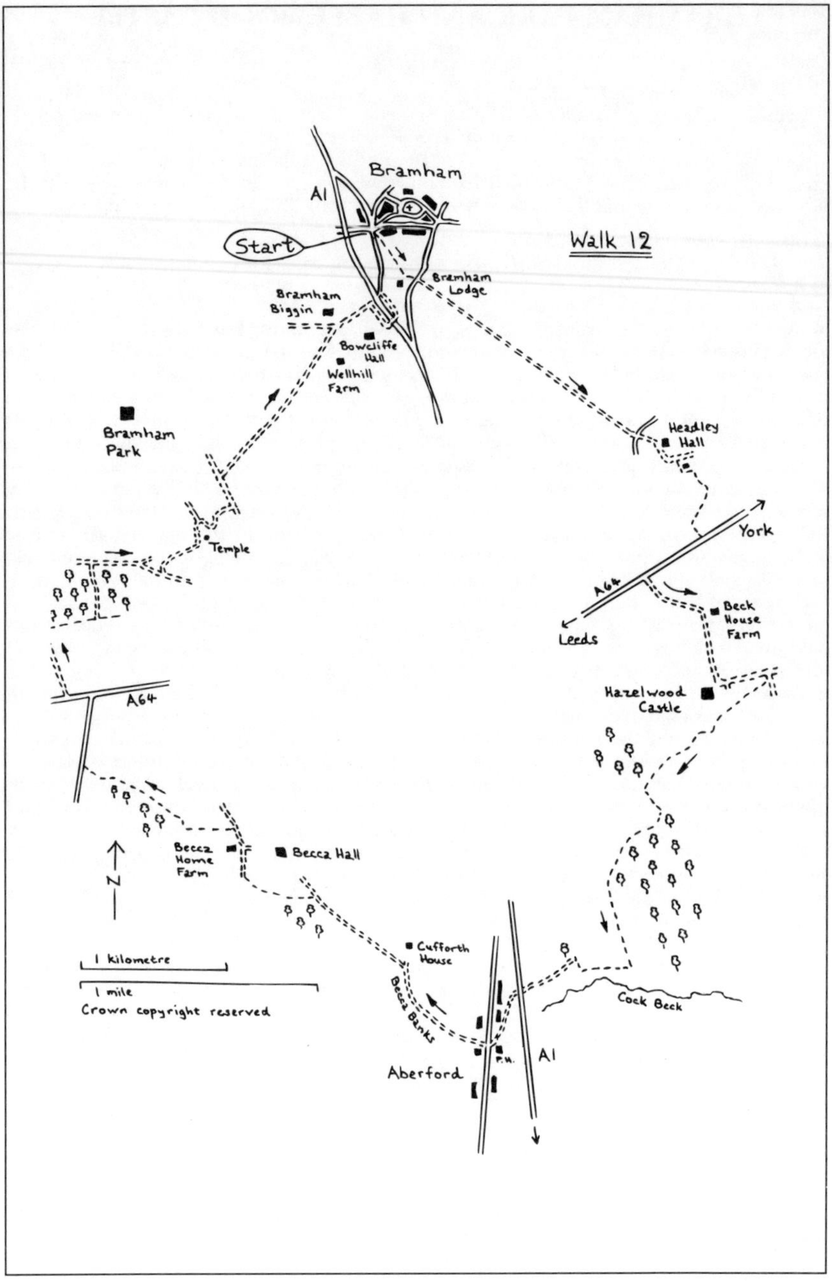
Bramham
A1
Start
Walk 12
Bramham Lodge
Bramham Biggin
Bowcliffe Hall
Wellhill Farm
Bramham Park
Headley Hall
York
Temple
A64
Leeds
Beck House Farm
Hazelwood Castle
A64
Becca Home Farm
Becca Hall
N
Cufforth House
1 kilometre
1 mile
Crown copyright reserved
Becca Banks
Cock Beck
P.H.
A1
Aberford

forward across the field towards a small wood ahead. When you reach it, turn left along the track and follow it to the A1. Cross this with great care (see note at start of walk) and follow the track and then the road into Aberford, reaching the main road by a small triangular green and the Arabian Horse pub.

Cross the main road to the tarmac lane between houses opposite (Becca Lane), which is an old access drive to Becca Hall. Pass through a pair of old stone gateposts. The Iron Age embankment of Becca Banks is to the left of the drive. Ignore the drive forking right to Cufforth House and when the tarmac ends keep forward along the unsurfaced track to pass a lodge. After some distance the wood on the left comes back to join the track, and at the end of this wood fork half-left off the track (waymark). Keep the wood on your left for a few yards, then walk forward to enter an avenue of mature trees which you follow to its end. Follow the track with a fence closeby on the left, pass through a gate, and now there is a hedge to your left. Pass Becca Home Farm, ignoring a track through a gate to the right and the farmyard to the left, and keep forward on the track for about 100 yards to where on the right of the track there is a marker post with a large yellow diamond: here turn left on the path down the middle of the field to another marker visible at the far side.

Cross the bridge, and ahead of you on a tree in the middle of the field you will see the next waymark. From the bridge turn left for 20 yards, then sharp right up to the tree, then straight forward to the next waymark. Keep the ditch to your left to reach a stile. Keep the fence and wood to your left, and when the wood ends follow the fence/hedge, soon going right with the hedge to a stile in the next field corner. Bear slightly left across a narrow strip of woodland into the next field, and bear left round the edge with a wood to your left. Pass through a gap in the remains of a facing hedge and keep on by the wood. You join a track, and near the far corner of this field there is a sleeper bridge and a stile. Now bear half-right diagonally across the field, not towards the prominent signpost you can see at the far side but to another slightly further left.

Cross the stile and turn right up the road to reach the A64 again. Go left along the verge for about 150 yards, then cross and turn right into a track. When you reach a pylon and a wood, a footpath sign points right over a stile by a gate and a clear path leads along the edge of the wood. You have now entered Bramham Park. Look out for a waymark pointing left down a track between a birch plantation and a conifer plantation. In the dip you cross the infant Bramham Beck. When the wood on the left ends turn right along a cross-track. Shortly after entering another wood keep right at a fork, uphill, but when the ground levels out there is another fork, where you must go left. When you reach an 18th century temple the track bears left and right and you have a view left towards the house. Keep on the track as it winds round, and soon once more you have a wood to your right.

When you reach a T-junction with a white gate to your right go left as directed by the signpost and waymark. At the next junction go right, and at the next (possible) fork by a wood keep forward with the wood to your right. Pass through a gate and bear right with the track towards Wellhill Farm, but keep left at the fork before you reach the farm, soon joining a tarmac access road. You are joined by the main drive to Bramham Park from the left and on your left is the fine house of Bramham Biggin. On reaching the A1 go right, turning left at the entrance to Bowcliffe Hall to cross the A1 by the bridge, then left again on the other side down a tarmac footpath, which leads to the road back into Bramham.

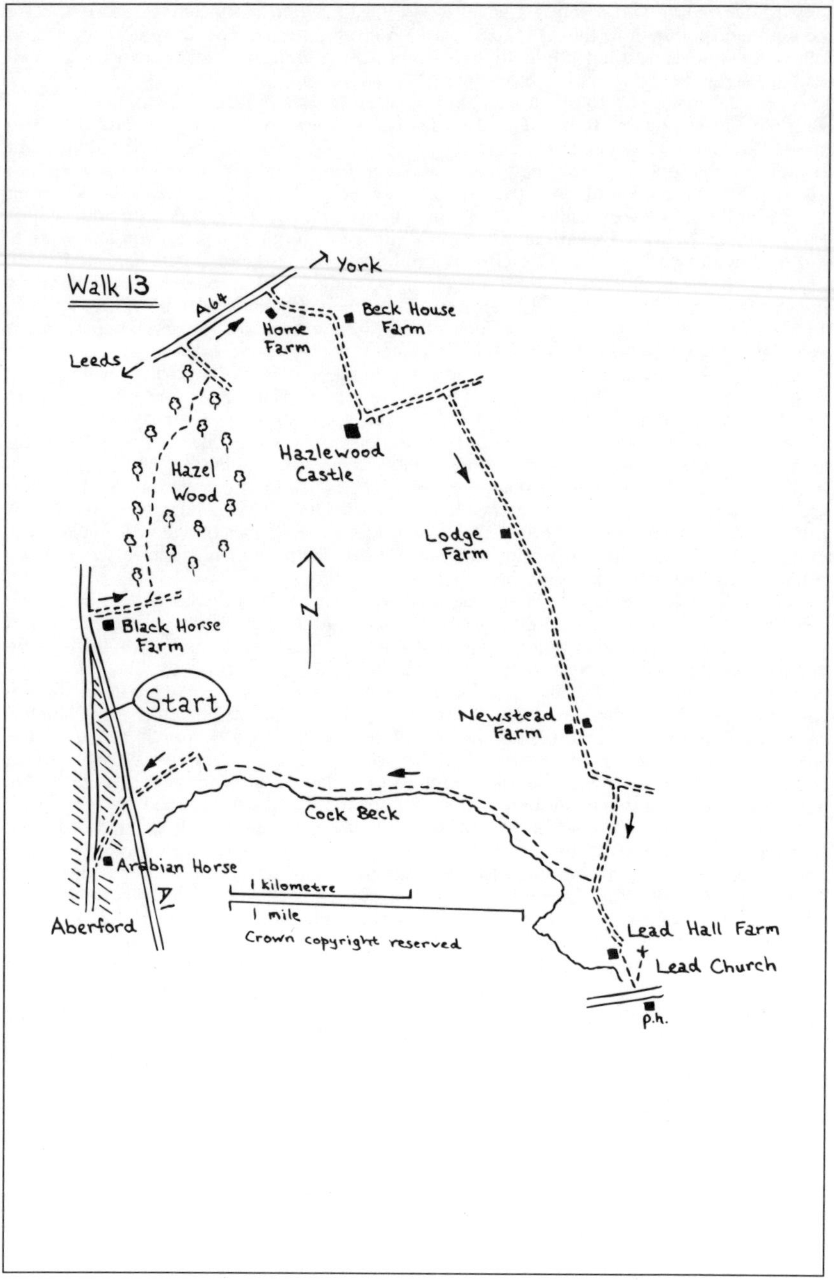
Walk 13
York
A64
Leeds
Home Farm
Beck House Farm
Hazlewood Castle
Hazel Wood
Lodge Farm
N
Black Horse Farm
Start
Newstead Farm
Cock Beck
Arabian Horse
Aberford
1 kilometre
1 mile
Crown copyright reserved
Lead Hall Farm
Lead Church
p.h.

HAZLEWOOD CASTLE AND LEAD CHURCH

WALK 13

7 miles (11 km); Pathfinder 684 (SE43/53), 673 (SE 44/54). Easy walking on good tracks and paths in the spacious countryside of the limestone belt. At present the route involves crossing the busy A1 twice, but when the A1(M) is built both places will be provided with a bridge or underpass, although there may be minor modifications to the route: look out for waymarks.

By bus: No. 64 from Leeds City Square to its terminus in Aberford.
By car: Park on the main street in Aberford and walk up to the north end of the village.

Continue walking up the old A1 away from Aberford until you reach the new A1, passing the old toll bar house on the way. Follow the footway beside the A1 for a short distance until you are opposite a break in the crash barrier between the carriageways. Cross the road here to the public footpath sign on the far side and follow the track between the buildings of Black Horse Farm. Having passed the last of the buildings there is another footpath sign and the track forks: keep left, towards a large pylon and the wood. At the corner of the wood another signpost points left and a narrow path leads diagonally into the wood.

Follow the clear path all the way through Hazel Wood. Wood anemones, ramsons and bluebells carpet the ground in spring, and an occasional patch of primroses has survived. When you reach a T-junction with a marker post turn left, and soon a stile by a gate leads on to the tarmac access drive to Hazlewood Castle. Turn left along it to the A64 Leeds to York road, then right along the grass verge for 500 yards to the next farm access road on the right, where a bridleway sign points to Hazlewood and Stutton. Follow the track until you reach the entrance gates to Hazlewood Castle, where you turn sharp left with the track, ignoring another track forking right a few yards further on. (It is worth having a look into the courtyard of the castle.)

Ignore the next farm access road on the right by a shed, but take the next one by a large sycamore tree, with a sign to Lodge Farm. The track leads straight past Lodge Farm and Newstead Farm, then dips and rises to a T-junction. Bear left here, but in 150 yards turn right again at the next junction, along a track with a ditch and hedge to the left. Top the next rise and drop into the following dip. At the lowest point you will notice a track forking right to a hedge corner: that will be our return route to Aberford. For the time being keep forward along the main track until you reach a gate at Lead Hall Farm. Pass through and walk down with the hedge to your left to a stile by another gate.

There is no right of way from here to the early 14th-century Lead Church in the middle of the field, so theoretically you must turn right with the hedge/fence to your right and follow it down to a large gate near the bottom corner, from where the right of way makes a beeline back across the field to the church. You may want to take the chance to call in at the Crooked Billet pub a few yards further on.

Now retrace your steps to the junction mentioned above and follow the track down to the hedge corner. Keep the hedge on your left along the edge of the field and soon you have Cock Beck to your left. The delightful path now essentially follows the beck, sometimes close to it, sometimes a little way off. Eventually you pass through a gateway in a facing hedge and now the path bears slightly right away from the beck towards the bottom edge of the wood. Follow the wood along to a stile in the field corner and bear slightly right up to a footpath signpost at a hedge corner.

Cross the stile into scrubland and follow the clear path parallel to the hedge on the right. Eventually the path bears right up the slope to a gateway in the hedge. Keep forward across the field towards a small wood ahead. When you reach it, turn left along the track and follow it to the A1. Cross this with great care and follow the track and then the road into Aberford, reaching the main road by a small triangular green and the Arabian Horse pub.

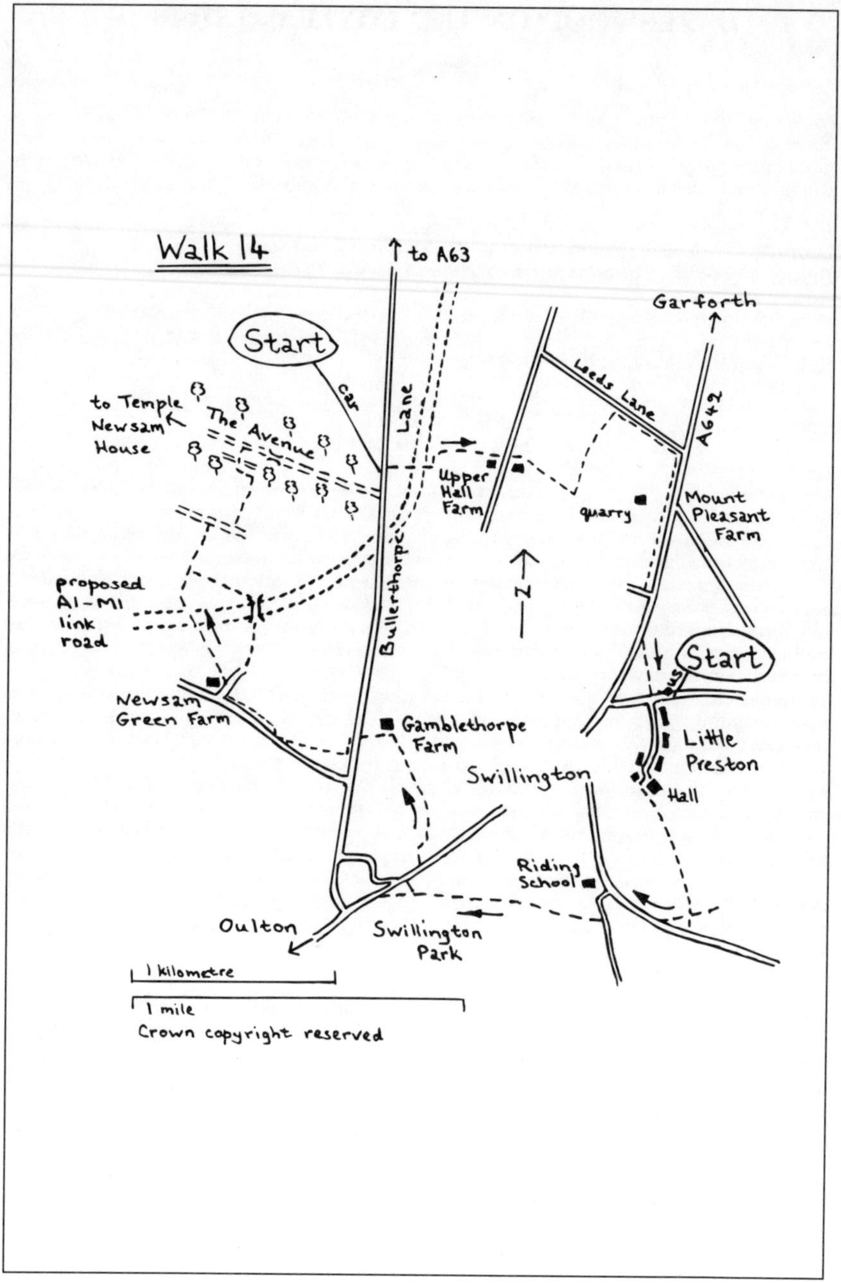

Walk 14
to A63
Start
Car
to Temple Newsam House
The Avenue
Lane
Bullerthorpe
Garforth
Leeds Lane
A642
Upper Hall Farm
quarry
Mount Pleasant Farm
N
proposed A1-M1 link road
Start
bus
Newsam Green Farm
Gamblethorpe Farm
Little Preston
Hall
Swillington
Riding School
Oulton
Swillington Park
1 kilometre
1 mile
Crown copyright reserved

SWILLINGTON AND LITTLE PRESTON

WALK 14

$5^1/_2$ miles (9 km); Pathfinder 683 (SE23/33), 692 (SE22/32). Old tracks and paths, a charming village, and a stroll through Temple Newsam Park. N.B. Construction of the new A1/M1 link road will make this walk impossible for a time, and once it is finished there will be minor modifications to the route: see sketch map and look out for waymarks.

By bus: No. 168, 169, 170, 468 Knottingley bus from opposite the Bond Street Centre on Boar Lane in Leeds to Goody Cross Lane, Little Preston. Alight close to Hall Road.
By car: Driving from Leeds towards Selby on the A63, shortly after you are joined by the A6120 Leeds Ring Road, there is a stretch of dual carriageway leading to a large roundabout by the Sainsbury superstore. Turn right here (signposted Oulton); the road bears left and reaches a T-junction: this is Bullerthorpe Lane; turn right along it and continue until woodland starts on the right and there is a wide gateway (into the Temple Newsam estate). Park here beside the road, walk back along Bullerthorpe Lane in the direction you have come from for about 100 yards to a signposted bridleway on the right and start the walk at [*] below.

From the bus stop walk back a short distance, turn left into Hall Road (a no through road) – you are now on the Leeds Country Way – and follow it down through Little Preston. The road ends at the Hall: fork right here, then bear left on a track round the outside of the Hall grounds. When the track bears right to a gate, keep forward on a narrow woodland footpath which leads to a cross track with a bank beyond. Turn right along the track to a large gate and a road. (Leeds Council intends to create an alternative route here avoiding the road: look out for waymarks.) Bear right along the footway as far as the next minor road on the left just before the Astley Riding School. The road is soon blocked by a pile of rubble, but pass round this and continue along the old road until you reach a signposted bridleway on the right. Follow this narrow path, which has old causey stones in places, along the old boundary wall of Swillington Park, until you join a better track, and bear right along this until a hedged path forks right off it. Follow this for 100 yards to the A642, here leaving the Leeds Country Way.

Cross to the footway opposite and turn right. A short distance past a bus stop a footpath sign points through the hedge on the left. The path follows the fence on the right. Follow the edge of the field until you reach a stile in the far corner. Cross and bear half left over the corner of the field to the hedge opposite and follow this up to the top corner of the field, where a narrow overgrown path between tall blackberry bushes leads to a stile. Bear left to a small gate, pass through the yard of Gamblethorpe Farm and follow the farm access road to the main road. Cross over to pass through a gate opposite and turn left along a fenced path, which can be overgrown.

Follow this path until another right of way turns right off it and follows a line of pylons over grassland, emerging onto a road at a barrier by a gate. Do not go through the barrier, but keep straight on along a path with a wire fence to the right and a hedge to the left, parallel to the road, even though this passes close to a very ugly household waste tip. Where the hedge on the left ends cross straight over the entrance into the tip and a few yards further on take the access road on the right to Newsam Green Farm.

[Look out for a waymarked diversion on the next section, once road-building is complete.] Now the ugliness is all behind you. In 60 yards cross the stile by a gate in the hedge on the left and bear half-right, keeping to the right of the buildings, to the next stile by another gate. Keep straight forward up the track, passing to the right of a large barn, to another gate, then on to the next stile by another gate and so along the track. Soon Temple Newsam house appears ahead. When the track ends cross the stile by the gate on the right and walk along with the fence to your right and a view to Leeds city centre on the left. Cross the next double stile and keep on along the field edge to the next stile, which gives access to a track.

Turn right along this, and a few yards before the track ends cross the stile on the left and follow the path towards the wood with a fence to your right. Enter the wood (and Temple Newsam Park) and reach a clear cross path; turn left along it, drop by old steps to cross a valley with a footbridge in the bottom, and climb the steps up the other side. At the top take the path forking right, cross straight over the next clear cross path and reach a broad straight cross track. This is the Avenue: turn right down it to cross a long stone bridge with a pond beneath it, and as you climb up again look back for a view straight to the front of the House. The Avenue leads back to Bullerthorpe Lane, where motorists should find their car.

If you have come by bus, turn left along the road for 100 yards to take the signposted bridleway on the right, and [*] follow the track (this section will also be affected by the new road) to the next motor road, Swillington Lane at Hollinthorpe, which you reach through the yard of Upperhall Farm.

Cross the road and take the track opposite, signposted as a public footpath, passing to the left of Hollinthorpe Low Farm. When the track ends at a field fork half-left along a hedged green lane. Soon you are faced by a huge quarry, owned by Swillington Brickworks, which has occasioned an extensive diversion of the footpath. Bear left along the edge of the quarry in a fenced path which can be overgrown. Cross a stile into a field and keep forward along the old hedge to a waymark post at the far end of the field, then straight on down the hedged lane to the road (Leeds Lane).

Just before the road there is a bench on the right with a stile behind it: cross this and walk along the lefthand edge of the field parallel to the road (no clear path). Garforth is over to your left. Cross two stiles and keep forward until beside a road junction the field boundary forces a right turn on you. Continue parallel to the road, now the busy A642. Cross another stile and keep on, now with Mount Pleasant Farm 120 yards to your right. In the next field corner cross a stile onto the farm access road and turn right along it for 50 yards to another stile on the left. Cross this and walk forward along the edge of the field with a fence to your left. Soon you are on a raised bank again parallel to the main road. At the end of the field drop down the bank and cross the stile, mounting a few steps to the brickworks access road, thus ending the diversion caused by the quarry!

Turn left to the main road, cross it to the footway opposite and turn right. We are now back on the Leeds Country Way. Ignore a footpath sign on the left and pass a large metal wheel which indicates the start of Swillington. A few yards beyond this the footway changes to the other side of the road, but just before it does fork left off it and walk along the righthand edge of the field with a drop to a beck on your right. Follow the field edge to a stile in the hedge at the far end, then keep on with a hedge to your left, now on a clear path. Cross the next stile and follow the fence on your left to another stile and a road. Those who came by bus will recognise their starting point, motorists will cross straight over into Hall Road and return to the start of the walk description.

GREAT AND LITTLE PRESTON, KIPPAX AND THE RIVER AIRE

WALK 15

6½ miles (10 km); Pathfinder 683 (SE23/33), 684 (SE43/53), 692 (SE22/32), 693 (SE42/52). Unfortunately on this ramble a certain amount of pavement walking is unavoidable, but it is hoped that the quality of the footpath sections will more than compensate for this. For ornithologists the wetland area by the river should be particularly rewarding, and for botanists the Townclose Hills SSSI has a wealth of wildflowers.

By bus: No. 168, 169, 170, 468 Knottingley bus from opposite the Bond Street Centre on Boar Lane in Leeds to Goody Cross Lane, Little Preston. Alight close to Hall Road.
By car: Driving from Garforth to Swillington on the A642 look out for a left fork signposted to Great Preston and Allerton Bywater: this is White House Lane and there is a picnic area 300 yards along it on the right; park here, return to White House Lane, turn right along it and start the walk at [*] below.

On the opposite side of Goody Cross Lane from Hall Road there is a stile: cross it and follow the fence on the right to another stile. The clear path now stays close to the righthand edge of the field to a stile in the hedge ahead. Keep forward along the lefthand edge of the next field with waste ground and a drop to the left. At the main road bear right along the footway. Pass the brickworks entrance and, on the right 100 yards further on, just after the first trees, look out for an unmarked stile and cross it, bearing left up the grass to a picnic area and car park. This is where those doing the walk from their car will have parked. Bear right at the car park to reach White House Lane and turn right along it.

[*] You are on the Leeds Country Way. In 120 yards fork left by the footpath signpost, cross the ditch by a footbridge and enter a hedged track. It makes a sharp turn right, then another one left, and reaches the tarmac Brecks Lane over a stile. Turn right and follow it past the large Brecks Farm. Keep left at a fork. The track drops past Brecks Wood and crosses Kippax Beck before climbing to Kippax. On the way up you cross the track of a disused railway (the Leeds Country Way goes left along it). Continue uphill, and where the houses and the tarmac road begin turn right along Green Lane.

Walk along Green Lane until the houses end and then keep forward along the hedged bridleway. Ignore a footpath crossing from left to right. The path broadens into a track and reaches a tarmac road. Keep forward and where the road bends left follow it for a yard or two, then fork right off it along the signposted bridleway. When you reach the open grassland of Townclose Hills (a SSSI) you will find in summer a riot of wildflowers and a plethora of footpaths: explore them at your leisure, but our route forks right on a clear path. There are fine views right as the path contours round the hills. When you reach a clear fork keep right on the level contouring path.

The path bears left and you come to an open space; looking right over the valley of Kippax Beck you will see a wood with a tall pylon in the middle of it; at this point drop right on a clear path (i.e. in the direction of the wood), and at the next junction bear left along a level path towards another pylon. Keep always on the clearest, most level path and you will reach an area of open grass with the pylon 60 yards off to your right. Stay on the contouring path, roughly parallel to the power lines, until it drops to reach the line of an old hedge. Keep forward to reach the lawn behind Kippax Leisure Centre and walk along the lefthand edge of this to join a track which leads to the road.

Turn left along the pavement towards the centre of Kippax. The road climbs, and where it bends left you will see on the other side, just beyond Brigshaw Lane, a footpath sign pointing right down a tarmac ginnel. Follow it to the first cross street, where you go left for 80 yards to find the continuation of the ginnel on the right. The tarmac surface soon ends, but the path leads forward towards a pylon, passing to the left of it. Follow the clear path until you cross Kippax Beck again by a footbridge. In a few yards keep right at a fork, to follow a hedge on the right up alongside school grounds. The narrow hedged path can

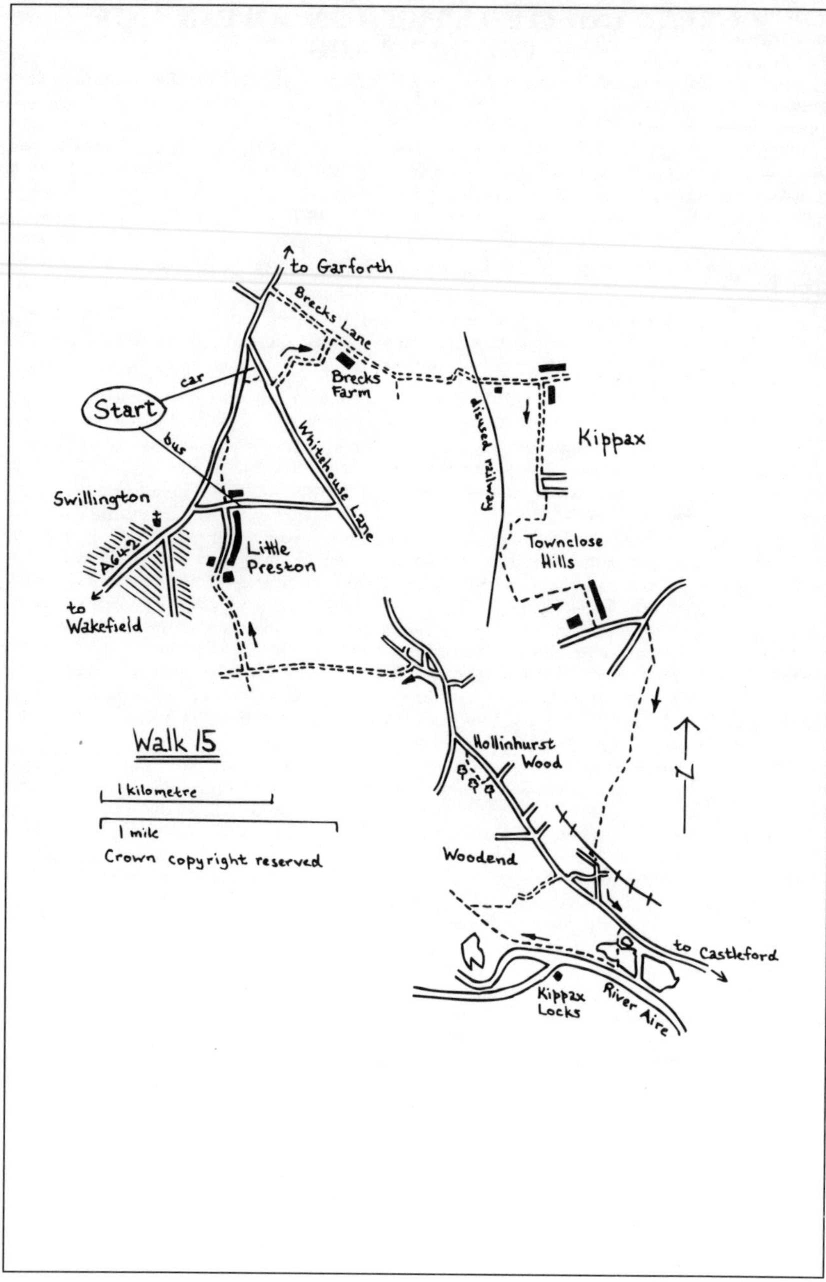

to Garforth
Brecks Lane
Brecks Farm
car
Start
bus
Whitehouse Lane
disused railway
Kippax
Swillington
A642
to Wakefield
Little Preston
Townclose Hills
Walk 15
1 kilometre
1 mile
Crown copyright reserved
Hollinhurst Wood
Woodend
N
to Castleford
Kippax Locks
River Aire

be overgrown. The path widens and at the end of the school grounds reaches a cross track. Keep forward on the path which soon leads through a tunnel under a railway to reach a cross track at the back of houses.

Turn left along the track, which soon bears right away from the railway. Ignore side streets to left and right and keep forward to reach a main road. Cross to the pavement opposite and turn left. Immediately before the filling-station take the signposted footpath on the right. Pass through a kissing-gate and keep forward. A notice-board informs you about what you might see in these Lowther Washlands. The path leads through this attractive wetland area to the floodbank of the River Aire: turn right along it. Kippax Locks will soon be seen on the other side of the river.

The right of way along the riverbank ends at a kissing-gate. West of here the rights of way are no longer as they appear on the map, so we shall have to make a detour through Woodend. Go through the gate and turn right, parallel to the fence on your right. To the left is a large lake popular with anglers. Cross a shallow valley by a wooden footbridge and keep on by the fence. Our way continues through a gate on the right by a footpath sign and along a fenced path, but you may like to make a detour left down to the lake.

The fenced path emerges onto a track: bear slightly right along it and follow it to the main road. Turn left. Ignore the Leeds Road forking left and keep forward along Preston Lane. Just after an iron wheel marking the start of Great Preston a wood begins on the left. This is Hollinhurst Wood, a SSI, and we can make a short detour through it. In a few yards a kissing-gate leads into the wood. Follow the clear path through the wood, and when you reach a path junction turn right. At the next T-junction, with two low stumps like gateposts on the right, go left, but a few yards further on fork right, to return to the main road opposite a school. Cross the road and turn left.

Wood Lane comes in from the left and you pass a War Memorial. Ignore Berry Lane on the right, signposted to Kippax and Garforth. You are now in White House Lane, which could be followed all the way back to the start, but a much more rewarding route is that through Little Preston. So turn into the next street on the left, Whitehouse Crescent, and where it bears right keep forward along Whitehouse Avenue. About 60 yards after this junction take the signposted footpath on the left. When you reach a wooden barrier the path forks: keep right along a clear path. Ignore a path which soon forks right into the wood. When the wood on the right ends, the top of Swillington church tower comes into view half-right.

The path broadens to a track. Follow it until about 200 yards before it ends at a gate: on the left here steps lead up the slope to a stile, but we turn right along a narrow path with a beck to the left. We have now rejoined the Leeds Country Way. The path becomes a track and leads up along the boundary wall of Little Preston Hall, bearing right round it. When you reach the gate, with the Hall on the right, turn left up the road through Little Preston to the T-junction at Goody Cross Lane. (Motorists will now go to the start of the walk description for the route back to their car.)

TEMPLE NEWSAM

WALK 16

4½ miles (7 km); Pathfinder 683 (SE23/33). Many hours can be spent exploring the 1200 acre Temple Newsam estate, which contains a wide variety of landscapes from formal gardens to wild woodland; this walk is just a representative sample. (N.B. The slightly longer walk suggested below may be impossible during construction of the A1/M1 link road.)

By bus: *No. 27/27A from Leeds City Square to Temple Newsam (half-hourly).*
By car: *Park in the car park near Temple Newsam House.*

Make your way past the lefthand side of the house to the terrace at the front, from where the countryside through which you will be walking lies spread out before you.

With your back to the House, turn left and at the end of the terrace go down the steps signposted Stable Block. Keep the stables and the Home Farm to your left, where the tarmac drive forks keep left, and when there is a three-way split ignore the cobbled way going through a gate on the left and take the middle drive down through high rhododendrons. Just before you reach the large pond, fork left, leaving the pond down to your right; ignore two paths forking right to cross bridges, but at the next fork keep right, with a car park up to the left. Cross straight over the next cross drive (car park to the left, rose garden to the right) and keep along a valley bottom with the beck to your left.

The track leads through a kissing-gate. At the next junction turn right uphill; at the top of the hill you are joined by another track from the left and soon reach Colton. Eventually the track bears sharp left and reaches a road. Bear right up to the T-junction, then right again. By Colton Methodist Church kink right, then left down Meynell Road. At the bottom of the slope, opposite Woodhall Court, turn right down a signposted footpath between hedges. Cross a wooden footbridge, then straight over a track by stiles into a fenced path which can be overgrown in summer. Cross over another track by stiles and continue along the righthand edge of the field. The path bears half-left to cut the far corner of the field, and re-enters woodland by a kissing-gate.

In a few yards turn left, parallel to the edge of the wood. When the edge of the wood turns right, so too does the path, and where it goes left again, keep with it, ignoring a waymarked path straight ahead and another path to the right. Cross a wide brick bridge and fork left, a few yards further on forking left again into a field. Walk up the righthand edge of the field, and just before you reach the fence at the top, fork right back into the wood and take the clear path away from the corner of the fence through the wood. Ignore cross paths. Eventually your path emerges onto a broad cross track: this is The Avenue, and looking right you will see that it leads directly to the front of the House. But our route crosses straight over and enters the wood again on a broad path past a waymark on a tree stump. When the path forks, with another waymark between the branches, keep left. When you reach a clear cross path, turn right. You are joined by two paths from the left, and now you are near the lefthand edge of the wood. Shortly you must keep left at another fork, with a stump between the branches which once had a waymark on it, on a path parallel to the edge of the wood. Just before the path begins to drop quite steeply you reach a couple of old stone steps: fork left here and leave the wood on a path which keeps to the right of a fence.

There are fields to your left and an area of young trees to the right. The path leads up to a stile. Turn right along the track. There is a fine view to the House and to Leeds city centre in the distance. Follow the track until it bends left (ignore a track forking right here) then right again to cross a bridge over the beck and reach a corner of the wood. Now fork left off the stony track along a grassy one towards a fence, and when a firm track joins you from the right, bear left along it. At the next fork you have a choice of routes: for a slightly longer walk, keep left and follow the track until it passes through a gate onto a narrow tarmac road; turn right up this to the top; for a shorter route, keep right, parallel to the fence on the right; just before the track reaches a gate, bear left along to a smaller gate and a bridleway sign. Here the longer variant rejoins us.

Turn right to a kissing-gate and walk forward on the tarmac road towards the house. The tarmac goes through a gate and fizzles out, but before the gate bear left along a track with young trees on both sides. When a high hedge begins on the left, pass through it and cross diagonally through a formal garden past a small pond. Make your way round the back of the House and through another small formal garden to return to your starting point.

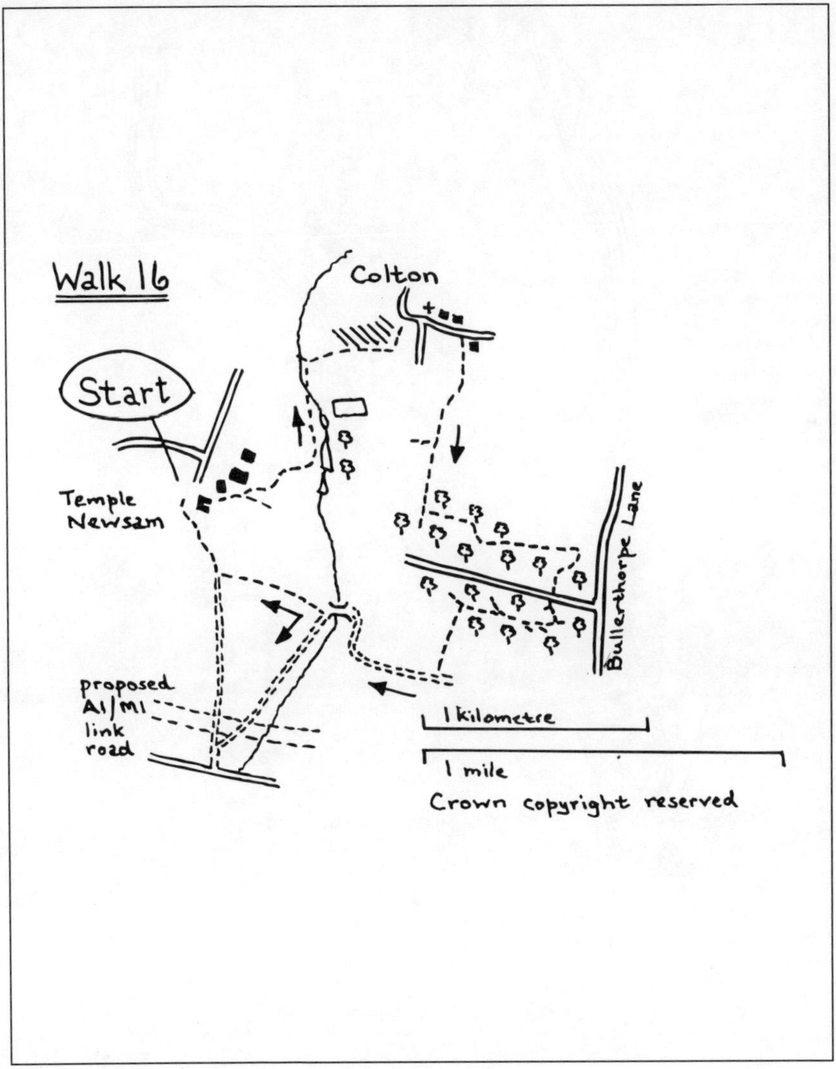

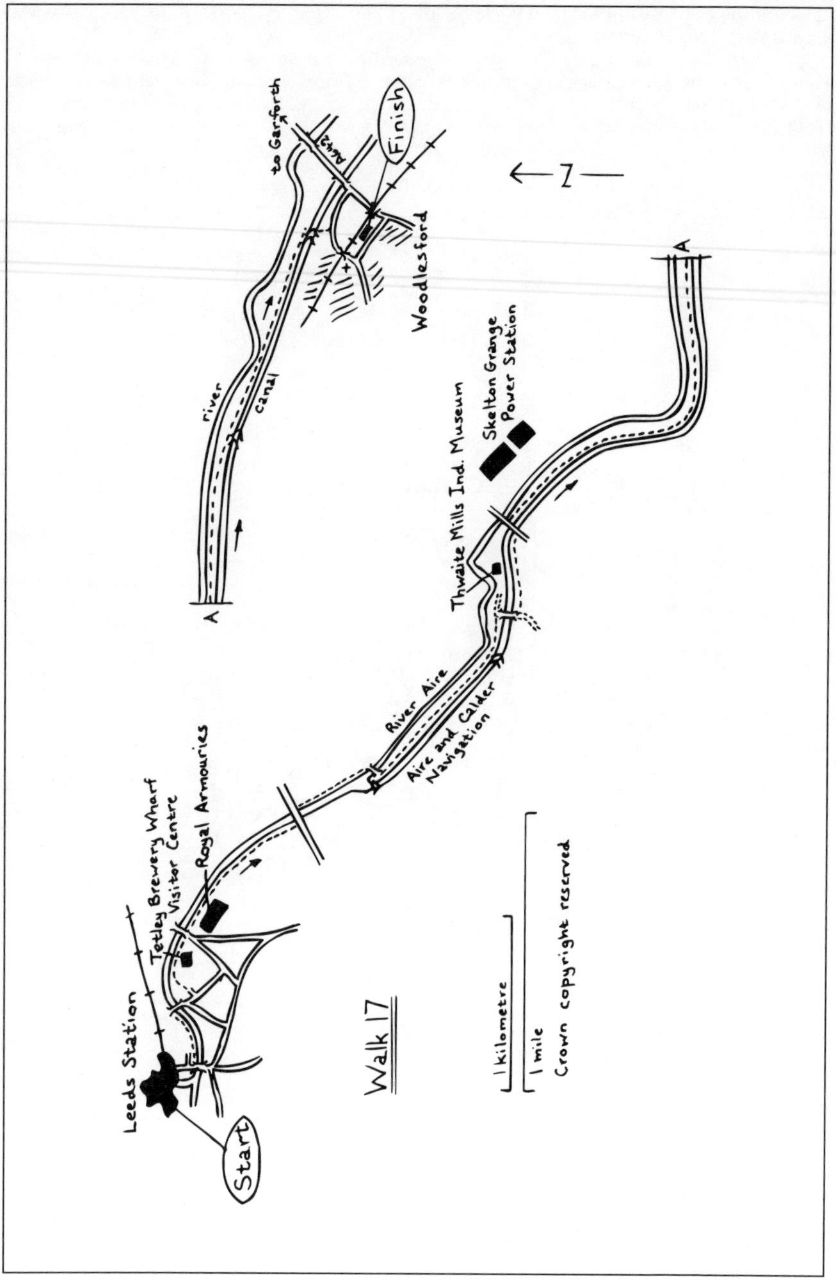

Walk 17
Leeds Station
Start
Tetley Brewery Wharf Visitor Centre
Royal Armouries
River Aire
Aire and Calder Navigation
Thwaite Mills Ind. Museum
Skelton Grange Power Station
A
A
river
canal
Woodlesford
Finish
to Garforth
N
1 kilometre
1 mile
Crown copyright reserved

THE AIRE AND CALDER NAVIGATION

WALK 17

6 miles (9½ km); Pathfinder 683 (SE23/33), 692 (SE22/32). A surprisingly attractive walk of great variety and much historical and wildlife interest; there is an opportunity to visit the Tetley Visitor Centre and the Thwaite Mills Industrial Museum. The walk is of course almost entirely level. Almost all of the route is part of the Trans Pennine Trail and is waymarked as such, but as there is still much construction work at the site of the Royal Armouries the actual route of the Trail is at the moment not walkable there; I have described the route as it is at present (November 1994), but please look out for the waymarks.

The walk, which is linear, starts at Leeds Station and the return is by train from Woodlesford (Hallam or Pontefract Lines). It would be possible to leave a car either at Woodlesford Station or Woodlesford Lock, take the train to Leeds and walk back to the car.

On emerging from Leeds Station walk straight over the pedestrian crossing to a small white tower building with a sign saying Way Out Bishopgate, go down the steps and turn right to follow the road under the station. Pass the entrance to Granary Wharf and the Hilton Hotel, then cross the main road at the traffic lights and continue your direction towards Victoria Bridge, but immediately before you reach it go through an iron gate and down some steps and turn left along the riverside path. Follow this round, across a car park and on to Leeds Bridge. Cross straight over the road (you may like to use the traffic lights a short distance to the left) and turn right over the bridge, noticing the plaque to Louis Le Prince on the first house on the other side. Pass the old offices of the Aire and Calder Navigation, now the North East Regional Office of British Waterways, and turn left along Dock Street.

Bear left along the cobbled Navigation Walk and soon go right along a pavement through a new housing development, which makes effective use of as much of the old warehouses as possible. Ignore a stout wooden footbridge and reach the river bank again. Follow it to the Tetley Brewery Wharf Centre. The route should keep by the river to Crown Point Bridge, pass under it and follow the broad paved footpath up past the bollards to turn left over the bridge then drop down a new ramp to regain the towpath, but due to building works it is necessary at present to pass right round the outside of the Tetley Centre away from the river to reach the Bridge, cross over the main road (Crown Point Road) and head along the road opposite towards the Royal Armouries development. Immediately after crossing a small bridge descend a flight of steps on the right and turn sharp right to pass under the bridge, then bear right along the riverside path. Now your route-finding problems are over!

Pass under the green girder bridge (South Accommodation Road) and immediately turn right and climb the steps to the road. Turn right over the bridge and immediately beyond it turn right again to cross the grass and enter a waymarked gravel footpath. When this ends keep forward along the track, but where this widens to a tarmac open space just before a bridge over the river, find the paved footpath in the righthand corner which passes under the bridge and follows a fence and pipeline along by the river. Cross the river by the next footbridge, turn left down the steps (Knostrop Flood Lock is to the right) and follow the path between the river and the canal.

Pass the next lock by a weir and the remains of a railway bridge, and in a short distance keep right at a fork along a narrower footpath. Look out for a flight of steps on the right (ignore them and keep on along the path if you want to visit Thwaite Mills) leading up to a road, and turn right to cross the canal. When the road curves right turn left to cross a concrete barrier and pass through a gate. Soon there is a lovely view over the canal to Thwaite Mills. Pass under the next concrete road bridge and follow the path as it bears right and climbs the steps to the road. Turn right over the bridge, but as soon as you have crossed the canal (and before you cross the river) go through a gate in the white metal railing on the right and descend the steps, there turning right along the path once more between the river and the canal. The next tree-lined section is perhaps the loveliest on the entire route. The large power station to the left is Skelton Grange.

Pass through a gateway under a pylon onto a track. Follow it until it passes through another old gateway: here fork right along a disused railway track, but immediately before the concrete bridge over the canal fork left through the barrier and descend to rejoin the path by the canal. (N.B. This section will soon be diverted away from the old railway track so that you will continue by the canal and pass under the concrete bridge. Look out for waymarks.) Looking left you can see that the Aire has been straightened, and there is a fine view to Temple Newsam in the distance. Pass Fishpond Lock and follow the path all the way to Woodlesford Lock. Cross the canal by the farther set of lock gates and follow the track away from the canal into Woodlesford. Turn right at the next road, ignoring New Farmers Hill, and follow it up and over the railway bridge, then immediately turn left for the station.

WOODLESFORD AND METHLEY

WALK 18

5½ miles (9 km); Pathfinder 692 (SE22/32). Riverside and field paths through surprisingly attractive countryside, including a section of the Leeds Country Way. At the time of writing major engineering works on the River Aire are taking place, but a permissive bridleway allows the circuit to be completed.

By train: Leeds to Woodlesford (Hallam or Pontefract Lines).
By car: park at Woodlesford Station.

Walk through the car park onto the road and turn left downhill to the A642; here turn left again and walk under the railway bridge. Cross the Aire & Calder Navigation, but a few yards before Swillington Bridge over the River Aire cross the road and take the track on the right signposted Leeds Country Way. Pass round a large metal gate and to the right of a derelict brick building, then bear right across a stile and walk along the river bank. Cross another stile and keep forward along a shaly path with a wood to the right. The path widens to a track and reaches a metalled track. Keep forward over the concrete bridge and pass to the left of a fenced area with large oil tanks. Pass to the right of a high wooden hide and follow the tarmac road as it bears right away from the river, still with the oil tanks to the right. Cross the Aire & Calder Navigation by Fleet Bridge.

Immediately turn left and descend to the towpath, then at once turn right between bollards (waymarked Trans Pennine Trail) along a gravel fenced track (this is the permissive bridleway) which soon bears left and proceeds between the railway and the development site. Eventually it drops and bears right under the railway. This is the old Fleet Lane, which you follow to the A639 in Methley. Turn left along the road and follow it to where it makes a sharp lefthand bend (there are sports fields to the left). On this bend take the signposted bridleway on the right, in a few yards bearing right at the buildings. A faint track continues forward through the fields, keeping a more or less straight line to the next road. It is not well used and can be overgrown. When you reach some trees, keep to the right of them, then forward along the old field boundary, again keeping to the right of bushes and trees, to drop to the road. Turn right. By the Mexboro Arms ignore the road on the right and the main road which bends left, and take the narrower Hungate Lane straight ahead.

Bend left with the road by the entrance to Methley Home Farm, and shortly before it bears left again take the signposted footpath through a barrier on the right and walk up the edge of the field with a wood to the right. The M62 is noticeable over to the left. Keep with the edge of the field, at one point making a sharp righthand turn, until 200 yards after the wood on the right ends look out for a plank bridge over the ditch on the right and a narrow path forward with a hedge to the left. At the far end of the field go right with the field edge and then slightly left again. In a few yards we join the revised route of the Leeds Country Way. When you reach a small wood projecting into the field, keep to the left of it, with the field boundary still on your left. When you reach a much clearer path through the wood, coming in from the right and bending off right again, ignore it, and keep forward down the lefthand edge of the wood and into the next field.

Continue down the edge of the field. Now you must pay special attention! About 150 yards from the wood, where the dense hedge on the left thins out, opposite the start of the houses over on the left, find a faint path forking left to cross a ditch by a concrete bridge. Now bear right on a clear path close to the righthand edge of this field. Pass to the left of a footpath sign and redundant stile and follow the field edge down. Oulton Leisure Centre and Oulton Hall appear over to the left. You reach the next road over a plank bridge in the field corner. Cross the road, go a yard or two right, then left into the field and along with a hedge on your left. About 30 yards before the far corner of this field cross a stile in the fence on the left and bear right down the edge of the next field to cross Oulton Beck by a footbridge. Continue forward to a kissing-gate, then on along the old field boundary to the next road.

Cross straight over, passing to the left of the bench on the corner, and take the minor road ahead. Follow this lane until it turns sharp left by some garages. Cross straight over the next main road to return to your starting point.

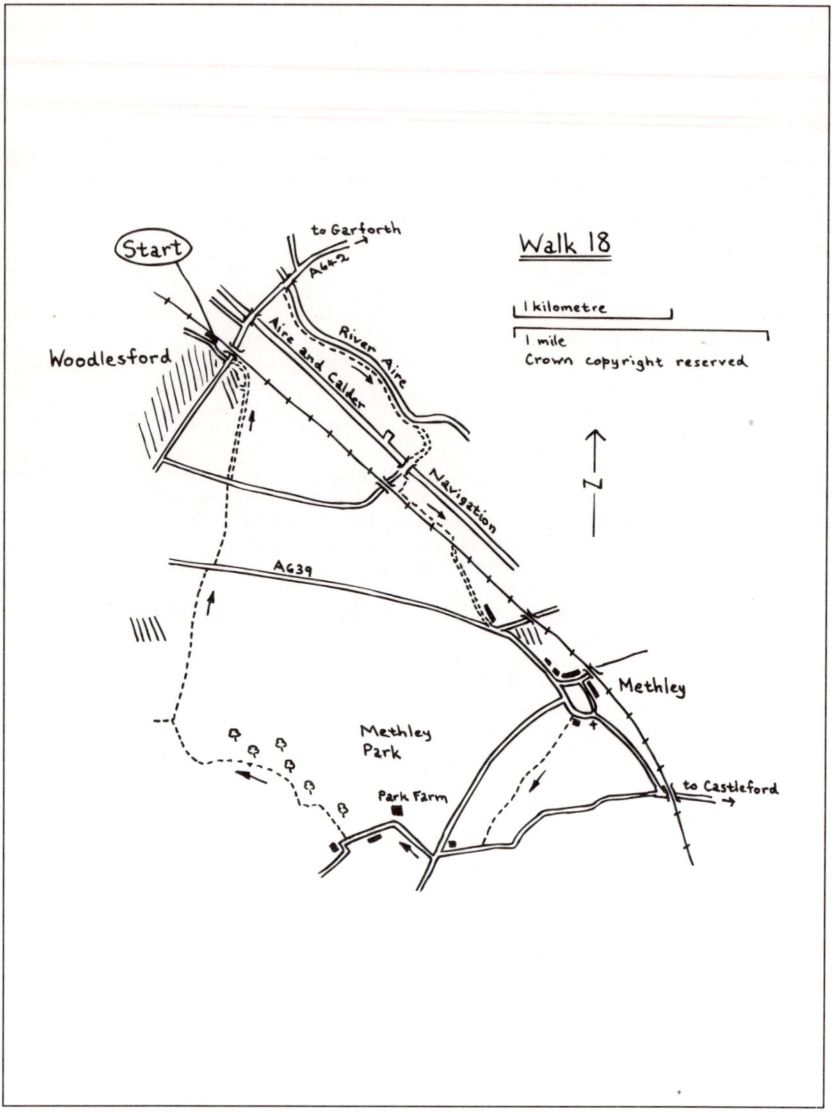

AROUND ROTHWELL

WALK 19

3¾ miles (6 km); Pathfinder 692 (SE 22/32). A mixture of attractive town ginnels and surprisingly rural paths and tracks, the climax of this easy ramble is what is probably the most extensive panorama of any walk in the book.

By bus: 7 from City Square, 167, 168, 169, 170 from British Home Stores in Boar Lane, 189, 410, 411, 445, 446 from the Central Bus Station to John o' Gaunts on the A639 Leeds to Pontefract road on the northern edge of Rothwell. The bus stop is a short distance before the John o' Gaunts pub, just after the start of the 40 m.p.h. limit. Cross the main road (there is a grass central reservation) and turn left along the pavement.
By car: In the centre of Rothwell, at the bottom of Church Street opposite the entrance into the Parish Church and the White Swan pub, there is a free car park. Park here, walk to the back corner of the car park to a tarmac footpath by the beck which leads to a kissing-gate and start the walk at [*] below.

Cross over the road leading right into the Industrial Estate, pass the Total filling station and follow the signposted tarmac footpath on the right with the high fence of Central Motor Auctions to the left. Where the path ends, cross over the pedestrian crossing by the entrance into CMA to find the continuation of the tarmac path, still with the high fence to the left. In a short distance the path ends and you must keep forward along the street to the next main road. Cross it and turn right. Cross Orchard Way and immediately after the next detached redbrick house on the left turn left down a tarmac ginnel. Shortly after passing a school on the right the path leads into a narrow street.

Keep forward, ignoring Churchfield Road on the right, then St.Christopher's Avenue on the left, but turn right along Gillett Drive. Where it curves right keep straight forward along a hedged footpath, and where it ends at a track keep forward along this to the next road. Cross over and enter the churchyard and follow the paved path to the main entrance to the church (the south porch). Turn left down the paved path to leave the church grounds by the lych-gate (the White Swan is to your left). Turn right to cross the main road to the car park, where motorists will find their cars. In the far corner of the car park a tarmac path with the beck to the left leads to a kissing-gate.

[*] Pass through the kissing-gate into Rothwell Pastures (Information Board) and continue along the grit path parallel to the beck. Soon the scant remains of Rothwell Castle can be seen over the fence on the right. Follow the grit path to a fork, and take the left branch which leads over two footbridges in quick succession. A few yards after the second bridge, at the path junction, take the path on the right parallel to the beck on your right. When the path bears left away from the beck to another junction, ignore a white footbridge down on the right and walk forward across the grass for a few yards to reach a broad cross path. Turn right along this and follow it to where it ends at a barrier and a road.

Turn right over the bridge and follow the footway towards houses. Immediately beyond the houses on the right, turn right along a broad track and follow it for about 200 yards, then turn left along an unsurfaced track at right angles to the first one. When you reach houses again cross straight over the tarmac street and keep forward along the footway by the track. At the next street, Northfield Place, cross straight over and follow the tarmac path through bollards to reach the disused railway line. Turn right along it. In a few yards take the left fork, and just before you reach a broad open space bear left along a narrower track, and in a short distance fork left off this one along a clear footpath with a hedge to the left, which follows a disused railway through a deep cutting.

On emerging from the cutting you reach a cross track: turn right along it, but in about 30 yards fork left off it down a clear path with an old hedge to the right. Ignore all paths forking left and right and follow the path forward eventually to pass through a barrier by a large gate onto a street. Continue on up the street, and at the main road (Wood Lane) cross diagonally right into a hedged track (bridleway sign). Cross straight over the next street and continue along the clear path. Your route is now as straight as a die all the way to the Leeds Road, sometimes as a path, sometimes a track, and in one place a narrow tarmac road. When the houses are left behind you have a vast panorama to your left, which includes the city, Skelton Grange Power Station and Temple Newsam.

Turn right along the footway by the main road. Those returning to Leeds by bus will find the stop opposite the John o' Gaunts pub, motorists will go back to the start of the walk description and continue from there.

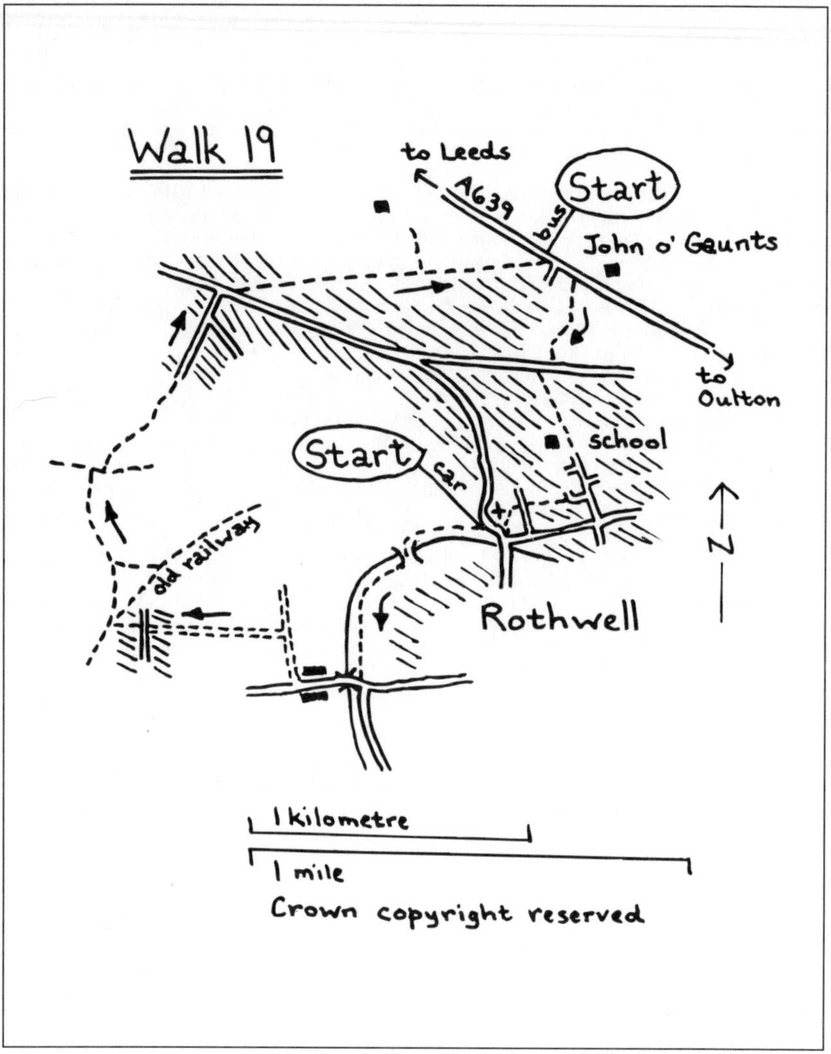

MIDDLETON PARK

WALK 20

3¾ miles (6 km); Pathfinder 692 (SE22/32). Mainly easy woodland walking in one of the major parks of Leeds; much of the route is on the South Leeds Heritage Trail, for which leaflets are available in the Ranger's Office (Lakeside Centre) in the Park, and the walk includes a visit to the 15th century Stank Hall Barn.

By bus: 76 from City Square (every 20 minutes) to the entrance to Middleton Park on Town Street, Middleton.
By car: Enter Middleton Park through the main entrance on Town Street, Middleton and immediately fork right to drive down to a large car park on the left. Return on foot to the park entrance.

Enter the Park and immediately fork left along a broad tarmac drive. To your right through the trees is Middleton Golf Course. Pass the South Leeds Heritage Trail Information Board No.11, and now you have the golf course on both sides. A short distance further along fork right through bollards along a gravel track and soon you reach tall rhododendrons on the left with a hedged enclosure behind. This is the Rose Garden: when you reach the entrance turn left into it. Diagonally right from this point, in the far corner, is an exit by which you should leave the garden again after looking round it. Pass a bollard, cross straight over a tarmac cross drive, pass a golf course tee and walk down the slope towards the golf course. But before you reach it turn right on a clear path through the trees, cross over a cross path and walk forward on a clear path which passes to the left of another tee into the wood. You reach a junction of tracks and a footpath signpost.

Follow the signpost to the right in the direction of Beeston along a paved path. This is Gipsy Lane. When the paving ends keep forward through the South Leeds Golf Club car park and about 100 yards beyond it turn left off the track by the signpost to Stank Hall Barn. Walk forward with an old hedge and trees to your left to reach rough ground. Continue over this to reach a cross track. The right of way keeps forward over more rough ground to reach the Beeston Park Ring Road down a flight of steps. Cross the road to find a flight of steps up the opposite bank. Up these walk forward with the old hedge to your left, and when you reach a golfers' cross track go slightly left and then continue forward with the old hedge now to your right, crossing several more golfers' cross paths. Now you must pass to the left of some blocks of flats, keeping forward over rough ground with no clear path between the golf course on the left and the fence round the flats on your right. Emerge onto a gravel track: turn right down it, then left over the railway bridge, to an Information Board and view of Stank Hall Barn.

Now return over the railway bridge and bear right up the gravel track, with views right to Churwell and Morley. When you reach a junction, the South Leeds Heritage Trail continues to the right, and you might like to explore this path for yourselves, but our walk keeps straight ahead, up towards houses, then bears left and climbs to the barrier onto Bodmin Road. Turn left along this, and soon curve right to reach the Ring Road again. Cross straight over and follow the gravel track opposite. In a few yards a signpost points left to Middleton Park. Where the track curves right, fork left off it along a paved footpath and follow this to the junction by the next signpost, a junction which is already familiar to you.

Walk forward along the broad track through the woods. At the next junction Information Board No.8 informs you that you are on the old route of the Middleton tramway. Walking on, you are immediately faced by a fork: keep left. Now ignore all cross paths, including one with a flight of steps on the right, and follow the old tramway down to the next Information Board, "City Vista". Don't follow the broad track ahead, with the fence of the Riding Centre to the left, but fork right through the wooden bollards on the track ascending through the wood. The track reaches a grassy area with football pitches.

Keep along to the left of these, with the wood on your left. At the T-junction turn left through bollards to a tarmac road and turn right down this.

The road curves left and descends to double wooden gates. By going left on the track a few yards before the gates you would reach the terminus of the Middleton Railway, but we turn right at this point along a tarmac track to re-enter Middleton Wood through an old gateway. Immediately after the entrance fork left, still on a tarmac drive, but you soon reach a marker post where you fork left over a plank bridge on a narrower path. At a fork keep right, i.e. straight on, and at the next junction, where there is a solid wooden marker post, bear right to reach a broad tarmac cross track. In front of you behind the tall hedge is the café. Turn left through metal bollards. In a few yards there are toilets on the left. Keep straight on to return to the car park and the main entrance to the Park, but it's worth going right along the front of the café to have a look at the lake, with a children's playground beyond, and calling in at the Lakeside Centre, the modern building behind iron railings, an information centre where leaflets are available.

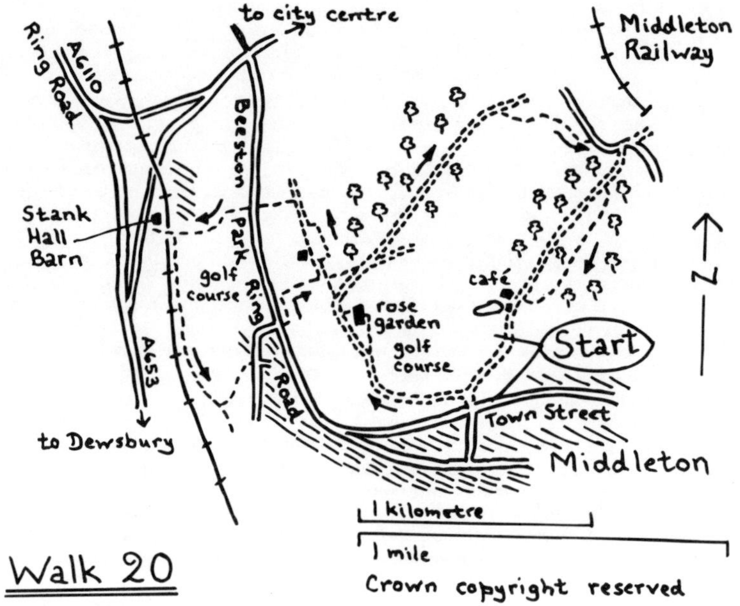

MORLEY AND CHURWELL

WALK 21

5 miles (8 km). Pathfinder 692 (SE22/32), 683 (SE23/33). The map has not yet entirely caught up with recent housing and footpath developments. A relatively rural ramble on the southern edge of the city.

By train: *Leeds to Morley (Huddersfield Line). Cross the line by the footbridge and turn left up the access road.*
By car: *Park at Morley Station (GR 270 282). If the station car park is full, there is room to park on the approach road from the town. From the car park walk uphill past the station on the left.*

The first few minutes of the route are not particularly attractive! At the top of the hill turn left along Valley Road, ignore the steep flight of steps at the end and turn left and then left again, to walk downhill, still with the station to your left. Continue past the Orcol fuel depot. Towards the bottom of the road fork right up a grit track with a high fence to your left. It bears round, and when you rejoin the tarmac track keep forward with a high wall to your left. When the tarmac ends continue forward, going left when the wall turns left, and cross the railway line (CARE!). Cross the ladder-stile on the far side and bear right along the track.

Now the quality improves, and you are in pleasant countryside. Soon your track climbs, to reach a cross-track on a bend. With Broad Oaks Farm over to your right, bear left along the track. There is a view right to the city centre, and the houses ahead are Churwell. The track bends left and then right again and climbs gently to reach the A643 at the south-western end of Churwell. Turn right along the main road. Pass All Saints Church and Shenstone Surgery on the right and Daffil Road on the left and 20 yards further on turn left up a signposted ginnel. The path passes between gardens and new houses. Just after you pass a wooden barrier the tarmac path bears left: fork right off it, downhill. Ignore a path forking right at a triangle of grass, and a little further on ignore another path forking right at another triangle of grass: bear left to reach a barrier and a road. Cross straight over and through another barrier and continue along this attractive path.

The path soon crosses a side beck by a footbridge. Climb gently through pleasant woodland to reach a tarmac cross-path and bear right down it to cross the beck and climb a flight of steps. Pass through a barrier onto a street of new houses: cross it and bear left. At the end of the street keep forward along a tarmac ginnel directly under the power lines. Cross the next street to find the continuation of the ginnel, and when you reach a tarmac lane turn right, then almost immediately left to cross the bridge over the M621.

At the next junction turn right along the tarmac lane and cross the stile by the large gate. Pass to the right of Hill Top Farm. Cross a stile and continue on the tarmac path, in a few yards meeting a concrete path coming from a tunnel under the M621 on the right. Turn left along a clear but narrow path. A few yards after the start of trees to the right of the path, go right at a fork and follow a clear path across the middle of the field. Well over the field the path bears left, to pick up a hedge which it keeps on its left. Follow this hedge until you reach a cross path, and here turn right, keeping a fence on your left. The path becomes a tarmac lane with the M621 above you on the right. Climb a locked gate and turn right to pass under the M621.

Turn right at the T-junction. The track bears left to a double gate and stile. Cross this and immediately turn right along a grit track. Where this ends, a clear path bears left towards the end of a hedge. Keep this hedge on your left, and ignoring a path forking left through it follow it until your path also leads through the hedge and up a bank ahead. At the top of this there are several paths: turn sharp left, up towards a fence, then bear left, keeping the fence on your right. When the path reaches a track, bear right along it, with allotments to your left.

Cross over the first street and keep forward along a ginnel. When you reach a cross path, bear left along it, ignoring a faint path straight ahead, and follow it to where it bears right, with the garden of Churwell W.M.C. to your right, and reaches a road. Turn right and follow the road up and round to the left to reach the A643 again. Churwell War Memorial is on your right and the Old Golden Fleece is across the road, also to your right. Cross the main road and continue forward along Little Lane. At the fork keep left, and immediately fork left again down a track. This leads to a stile by a gate. Cross this and keep forward along a clear path, heading for a stile in the distance. Cross this and bear slightly right, passing to the left of a power line pole, to reach a tunnel under the railway. Do not go through this, but leaving it to your left keep forward with a wall to your left for 25 yards, to where a path forks half-right across the large field, heading slightly to the right of a tall pylon and well to the left of the farm buildings. When you draw level with the pylon you reach a track.

Follow the track towards Broad Oaks Farm. Pass to the right of a large barn. Ignore a left fork to a bungalow, pass to the right of the farmhouse and keep forward along the track. When the track sweeps right, fork left off it downhill on a stony track, now back on your outward route, but where the track bears left at the foot of the hill fork right off it on a clear but narrow path across the field, towards a pylon behind some bushes. The path soon bears slightly left and climbs the slope, leaving a shallow valley to the right. Keep forward parallel to this valley (don't be tempted down into it), and pass an old stone gateway into a hedged way. When you reach a track keep forward along it, and eventually it becomes a tarmac road. There are fields on the left. Immediately before the houses on the left, turn left down a signposted track. It bears right, and Morley Station is down below on your left. At the next road turn left downhill to reach it.

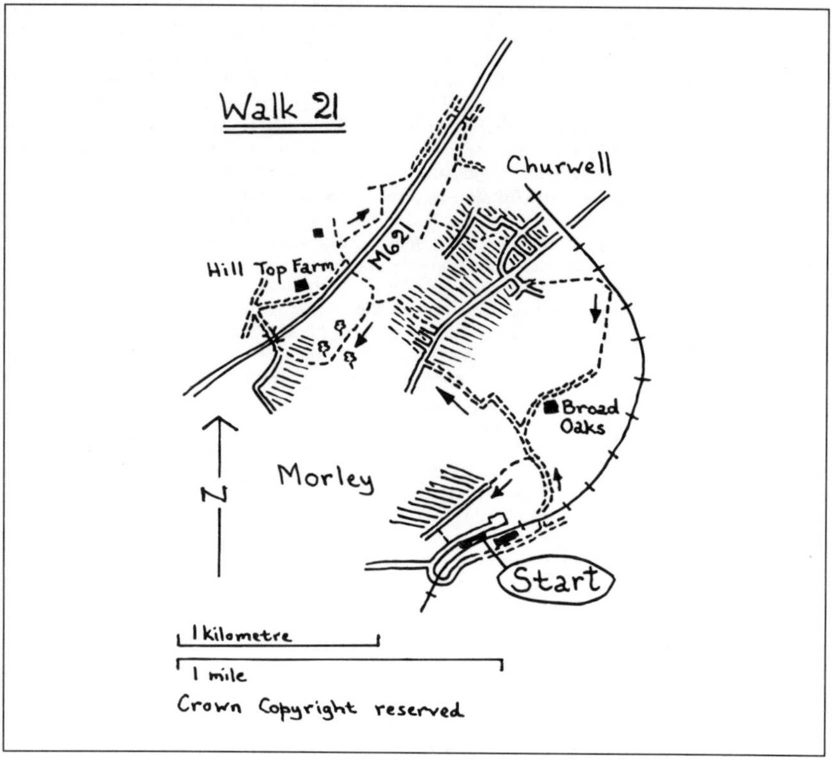

EAST ARDSLEY TO GAWTHORPE

WALK 22

6½ miles (10.5 km); Pathfinder 692 (SE22/32); easy, remarkably rural walk in the pleasant countryside south of Leeds, with an excursion into neighbouring Wakefield; includes a section of the revised Leeds Country Way.

By bus: No. 484 (Holmfirth) or 130 (Wakefield) from Leeds Central Bus Station (both are hourly). Alight in East Ardsley at the stop after the Bay Horse, just before the M1 roundabout.
By car: Follow the M1 south to Junction 41, the A650 Wakefield to Bradford road, and drive round the roundabout to take the Bradford road, but after a few yards turn right off it (care, it is a dual carriageway) into Royston Close, where you can park.

Walk for a few yards along the main road away from the motorway, then cross it and turn left into Stony Lane. When this forks keep left, i.e. straight ahead, and follow this lane past a farm until you reach a cross-track with an underpass under the M1 on the left. Go through this (you are now in Wakefield District), and at the T-junction at the other side turn right and climb to a stile by a gate, then bear left along the lefthand edge of the field. At the end of the high wooden fence on the left cross the stile on the left and turn right along a fenced path. The path bears left and passes through a kissing-gate. After the next kissing-gate the path bears left and then right to another kissing-gate into a fenced grassy way. Follow the fence on your left up, then cross a stile and keep forward, now with a tall hedge, then a high wall to the left. Cross another stile by a large white gate on the left and bear right up the access road. At the motor road turn right along the pavement and follow this pleasant country lane down into the dip then up to Kirkhamgate.

At the T-junction by the War Memorial turn left, and in 150 yards turn right down the signposted Gawthorpe Lane. Pass under the M1 again by another underpass. The track bears left and descends gently to cross Bushey Beck Bridge. You reach a farm access track on a bend: bear left along it, keeping the farm on your right. Ignore the next farm track on the right (which still has the old Leeds Country Way waymark, although it is no longer part of the revised Way) and when the lane becomes tarmac ignore another tarmac lane on the right. Keep forward to Gawthorpe, and leave North Ossett High School and its carpark on your right. About 100 yards further on turn right along a signposted ginnel, tarmac at first.

When the tarmac ends walk along the lefthand edge of the school grounds with a hedge to the left, but when the boundary of the school grounds bears right, keep straight forward along a narrow path, taking the first opportunity to fork left into a fenced path: bear right along this. Pass two redundant stiles and keep forward along the righthand edge of the field. Cross through two old field boundaries and continue along the righthand edge of the field. Cross the beck at the foot by a wooden bridge to the left of a concrete farm bridge, cross the stile and turn left up the fenced track. When you reach a cross-track, cross it and go through the lefthand of the two facing stiles, then turn right to follow the righthand edge of the field. Over the crest of the rise keep forward until the field edge bears away left. At this point keep forward with the fence to your right to a stile in the field corner.

Bear right down the righthand edge of the next field. In the bottom corner a track comes in from the left, again the old route of the Leeds Country Way. Ignore it, and keep on down the righthand edge of the next field. About two-thirds of the way down pass to the right of a redundant stile and as far as possible keep straight ahead – the path may be overgrown – still down the righthand edge of the field. Cross a stile in the bottom corner, go down a few steps and keep forward along the righthand edge of the next field, which soon curves right and then left again. Pass another redundant stile in the top corner and now bear slightly right over the next large field, keeping well to the right of the pylon and heading for the lefthand end of a hedge on the far side. At the hedge corner you meet a track coming across the field from the left: bear right along it with the hedge to your right. Cross a stile by a gate out of the field and walk straight forward down the tarmac lane.

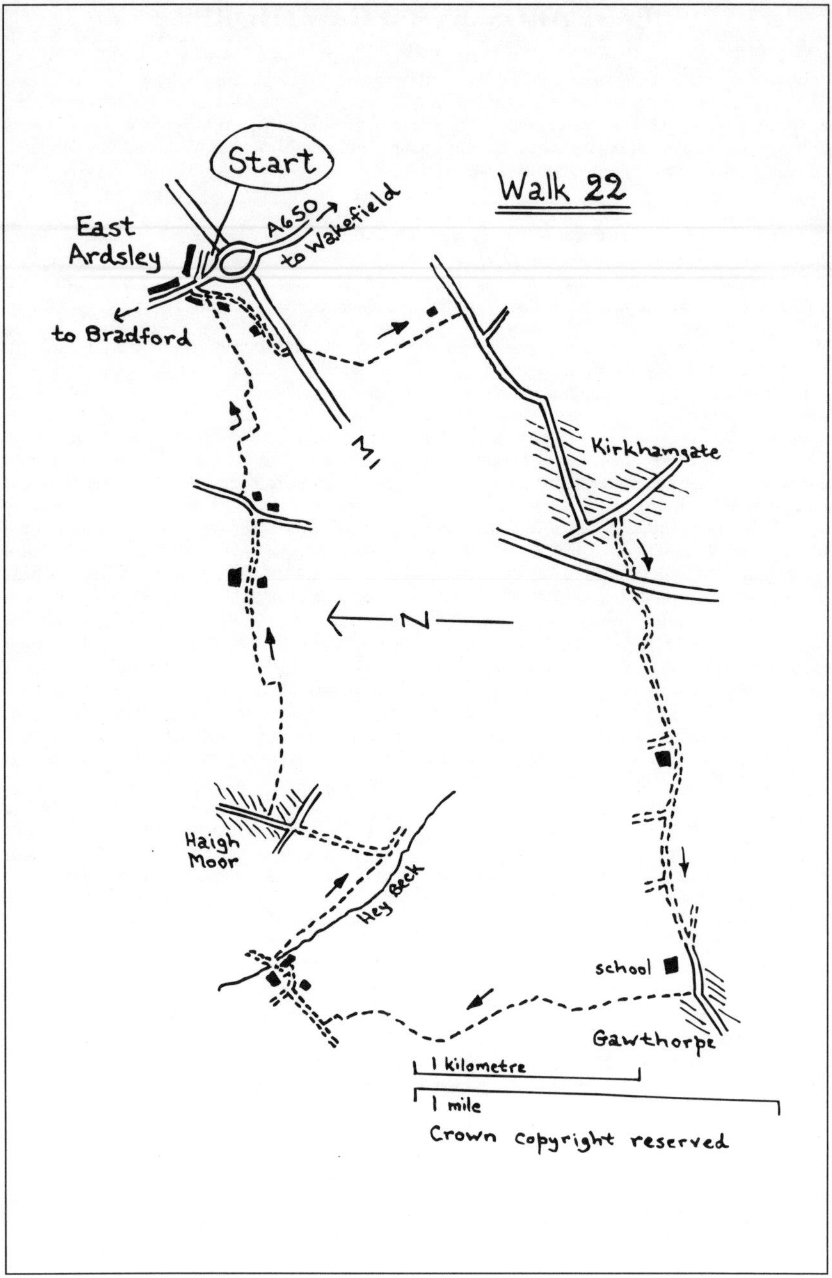
Start
Walk 22
East Ardsley
A650 to Wakefield
to Bradford
M1
Kirkhamgate
N
Haigh Moor
Hey Beck
school
Gawthorpe
1 kilometre
1 mile
Crown copyright reserved

The track bears left then right through the farmyard, and at the far side bear slightly right to find a footbridge over Hey Beck. At the far side of this turn right, soon reaching a stile into a field, and walk along the righthand edge of this. You are now back on the definitive route of the Leeds Country Way and back into Leeds District. Following the fence on your right you will soon spot a redundant stile at the righthand end of a broken-down fence ahead. Pass this and keep straight forward through the next field, keeping to the left of the trees and the top edge of the bank, and you will soon see the next stile ahead, where a hedge coming down from the left meets a fence by some tall trees. Bear very slightly right across the next large field: the next stile is in the far righthand corner of the field just in front of a small redbrick building. Cross the stile and turn left up the track.

When you reach the main road at Haigh Moor cross over and walk up Haigh Moor Road opposite. About 20 yards past the Methodist Church turn right along the signposted track. When this bears left, cross the stile ahead and walk along the fenced path. At the end of this cross the stile and keep forward along the lefthand edge of the next field. You are walking parallel to power lines. Cross the stile in the next field corner, cross over a track and continue forward into an old hedged footpath. At the far end of the field keep forward: the path drops then bears left, before turning right over a footbridge to a stile. Walk up the righthand edge of the field, cross a sort of terrace and another stile, then continue up the righthand edge of the next field. Ardsley Reservoir is over to your left. Cross the next stile to the right of two large gates and follow the track forward to the next motor road.

Turn left along the road. Soon it bears left and on the right are imposing iron gates into a modern house. A few yards further on is a signposted footpath on the right. Walk down the few steps and forward with a fence to your right. When the fence bears right keep straight forward across the field to a track where there is a marker post. Go right along the track for a few yards to find a clear path on the left heading over the field to the next marker post on the far side. When you reach this turn right down the edge of the field, to meet another track: turn left through the large double gates and follow the fence on your left to a stile. Cross it and keep forward with a hedge to your left; when the hedge ends, keep straight forward across the field to a stile in the fence on the far side just to the left of some bushes. Cross the stile and bear slightly left over the next large field, to find a stile into a fenced path just to the left of a house. At the end of this path turn left up the track, and now you have rejoined your outward route and reach East Ardsley in a few minutes.

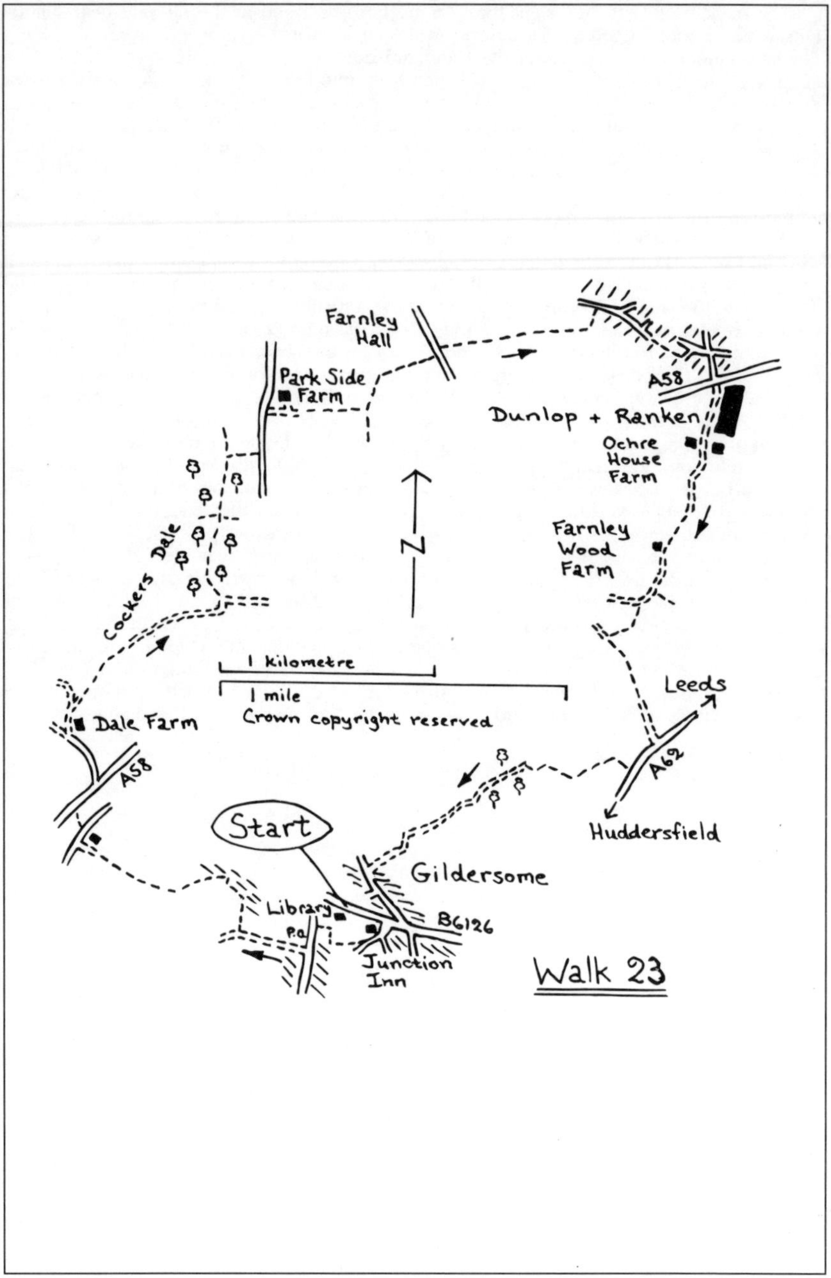

Farnley Hall
Park Side Farm
A58
Dunlop + Ranken
Ochre House Farm
N
Cockers Dale
Farnley Wood Farm
1 kilometre
1 mile
Crown copyright reserved
Leeds
Dale Farm
A58
A62
Start
Huddersfield
Gildersome
Library
P.O.
B6126
Junction Inn
Walk 23

GILDERSOME TO FARNLEY

WALK 23

6 miles (10 km); Pathfinder 692 (SE22/32), 683 (SE23/33); some built-up areas, but plenty of fine countryside with remarkable views; a section of the Leeds Country Way.

By bus: *No. 217, 219, 221, 229 from Leeds Central Bus Station to Gildersome Library.*
By car: *From Leeds follow the A62 Huddersfield road until the B6126 to Gildersome is signposted on the right; in about 500 yards a green will be reached, with benches; there is no official car park, so park sensitively near the green (GR 246 291).*

If you have come by bus walk back a few yards, with Gildersome Hall on your right, past the telephone kiosk, the pillar box and the toilets, and with the green ahead bear half-right, then right again past the front of the Junction pub. Ignore a footpath sign just past the Co-op pointing left, but 50 yards further, just before you reach a chemist's shop on the right, fork right along a cinder track, and a few yards further on, left into a ginnel. Soon there is a sports field on the right. The ginnel turns sharp right, then sharp left again, to reach the next main road. Turn left, but cross the road and just past the post office turn right along a tarmac lane. You have now joined the Leeds Country Way. The tarmac is succeeded by a dirt track between hedges. Where tracks come in from both left and right, keep straight on, but at a fork 100 yards further on keep right, following the waymarks. The track bears right and heads for the houses. There is a fine open view left to Drighlington. Soon you have the gardens of the houses to your right. Keep along the edge of the gardens until you pass through a squeeze-stile, then turn left through a barrier and keep on down a clear path.

Having come to the end of the houses the path continues with a hedge to the right, soon dropping quite steeply and bearing left to cross a stile and the valley of Andrew Beck, which emerges here from the ground at a spring. Climb the steps on the far side and bear right at the signpost. Now bear half-left across the field, away from the valley, to a prominently marked stile in the fence ahead. Having crossed this, keep forward with the fence to your right, but look out for a stile in it, cross this and bear left, now with the fence to your left. The next corner can be muddy. Follow the fence until you reach a gate in it, pass through and head up towards the farm with a fence on your left. When you reach the buildings cross a stile, then the yard, and walk down a few yards of lane to a motor road. Turn right, but in a few yards cross the road and fork half-left into a fenced path, which leads to the A58.

Cross and turn right. Immediately after the Valley Inn fork left down Dale Road. At the foot of the hill where the tarmac ends bear right over the beck and pass Dale Farm. After 100 yards fork right again through a stile by a gate, leaving the Leeds Country Way. Where the main track bears right into a field with a collection of farmyard antiques keep straight on, still on a clear track. The wooded Cockers Dale is down to your left. A short distance further on don't be tempted into the field on the right, keep straight forward, pass through an old gateway into a field and keep on with the hedge/fence to your right. Leave this field by a metal stile and keep forward on a clear path across the middle of the next field. Don't be tempted to fork left into the trees. Soon you are again following a hedge on your right, which leads to a stile by a gate and a walled lane. There is a nice view over Cockers Dale. Keep on the track until you reach the end of a small practice ground for pony jumping on the left and a T-junction.

Turn left through the kissing-gate and walk down the track. Ignore another kissing-gate on the left which leads to a path down into the woods, and keep on the clear contouring path with the steep drop to your left. Ignore a path forking right by a bench and a few yards further on ignore another one through a stile and down some steps on the left, and another waymarked path on the right a few yards after that. Keep on along the contouring path, but take the first clear path forking right (there is an iron fence corner close above you on the right) uphill, soon with the fence to your right, to pass through a stile at a junction of iron fences and follow a fenced path uphill to a stile and the main road.

Cross the road and turn left along the footway. In just over 200 yards turn right up the access road to Park Side Farm, but where it bears left to the farm keep straight ahead along a track. Pass through a stile and keep on along the clear path. Cross a stile in the next facing wall and keep on along the righthand edge of the field. Just before a wall starts on the right you meet a clear cross-path (the section to the right is paved); turn left across the middle of the field and at the high wall on the far side bear right to pass into a fenced path with the remains of paving and follow it to the next road. Just before you reach it a wide gateway on the left leads into Farnley Hall park, which you might like to explore.

But to continue the walk turn left along the road, in 50 yards crossing a stile on the right, just before a track leading to a sports ground, and walk along the lefthand edge of the field. Cross the next stile in the far corner and continue down the fenced path. Cross another stile and keep forward with the hedge to your left, at the end of this field crossing another stile, climbing up the bank ahead, then bearing half-right down it again onto a reasonably clear path which in 15 yards meets a cross-path, along which you bear left. Soon the path becomes clear again. Keep on with trees and a drop to your right, open ground to your left. The path becomes a broad track. When this begins to descend there is a good view over Leeds Ring Road in the dip ahead to Upper Wortley on the hill beyond. Keep forward down the slope to join a paved track coming from the left.

When you are faced by a metal fence turn left and follow the fence down. At the bottom turn right along the street and where it forks keep right along Cobden Road, heading towards the Dunlop & Ranken warehouse in the distance. This part of Leeds is known as New Blackpool. When the road bends left at Cobden Street keep straight forward with houses on the left and allotments on the right. There are traces of paving. Soon you pick up a tarmac path: follow it forward, ignoring paths sloping up the high embankment on the right, and follow it as it bears left to a T-junction. Turn right (Cow Close Road) and at the next T-junction again turn right, uphill, to reach the A58 again with the Dunlop & Ranken building immediately ahead.

Cross the main road and turn right. Turn left into the wide factory entrance (there is a footpath sign and a sign to Ochre House Farm farm-shop), bearing right in front of the warehouse, still along a road. Immediately before the last of the Dunlop & Ranken buildings fork right and enter the yard of Ochre House Farm. Follow the track through the yard, out the other side and on uphill (stiles are provided if the gates across the track are closed). From the top there is an extensive view back towards Leeds city centre. When you draw level with a large shed on the right, ignore the concrete track forking left through a gate, cross the stile ahead and keep on the narrower concrete track which bears half-left across the field. At another stile by a gate the concrete ends. Keep straight forward across the next field towards the lefthand end of the buildings of Farnley Wood Farm.

Leave the field across a cattle-grid and bear left for a few yards to the next stile. Continue down the tarmac access road. The next stile is to the right of its gate. Where the tarmac road bears right, cross the stile on the left and keep your previous direction across the field to pass under a double row of power lines and cross a stile in the fence ahead. The views are remarkably extensive. Bear right along the righthand edge of the field until at the end you meet a cross-track. Turn left on it downhill. At the foot it crosses Farnley Wood Beck and leads up through trees to a stile and the A62.

Turn right and walk past St.Bernard's Mills, a collection of workshops and warehouses, and 50 yards further on follow a footpath sign which points right into the field. Walk along the righthand edge of the field, but in 100 yards, by a wooden pylon, the path makes a sharp turn left and follows the line of pylons across the field. With two of the pylons still to go, the path bears half-right – it is a very clear path across this very large arable field – and soon bears slightly left again to reach the far side of the field close to yet another wooden pylon. Bear right along the edge of the field and in the next corner cross a sleeper bridge, then keep along the lefthand edge of the next field. At the far end of this field the path bears slightly left. Keep forward, ignoring a large metal gate on the left and a gateway opposite, cross the small beck ahead (there may be the remains of a sleeper bridge), pass to the right of a very large old stone gatepost and keep on the clear path along the old hedged track (to judge by the size of the hedges the path is of some antiquity).

Cross a stile, and sections of the path have a brick surface. A yard or two before a stile the path forks: keep right and cross the stile and the cross-track, and keep forward along the track opposite. This kinks left and right and continues up the slope, at first with the remains of a wall to the left. The track climbs quite steeply – there are long views back – and at the top you are joined by another track from the left. At the next clear fork keep left along a narrower path (the track leads down right to a farm), and soon the old hedged lane leads down past a converted chapel to Gildersome. Keep left down the hill to a T-junction and turn left to return to your starting point.

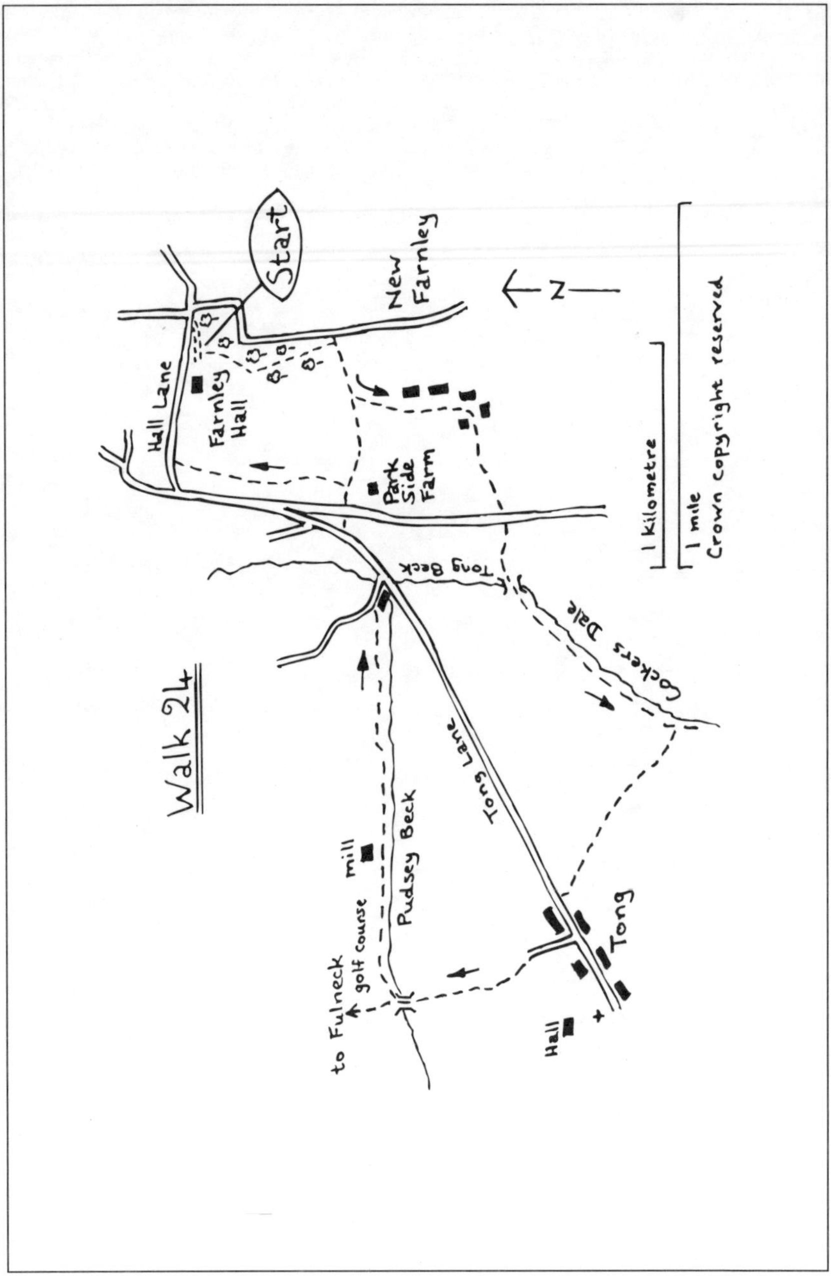

Walk 24
Start
New Farnley
N
Hall Lane
Farnley Hall
Park Side Farm
Tong Beck
Cockers Dale
1 Kilometre
1 mile
Crown copyright reserved
Tong Lane
Pudsey Beck
mill
golf course
to Fulneck
Tong
Hall

FARNLEY PARK, COCKERSDALE AND TONG

WALK 24

5½ miles (9 km); Pathfinder 683 (SE23/33); an easy ramble along field, woodland and beckside paths, many of them paved. Part of the walk is on the Leeds Country Way.

By bus: No 66, 66a, 67 from Leeds Central Bus Station to Hall Lane; walk back along Hall Lane and turn right into Farnley Hall grounds, continuing up the access road to the car park.
By car: Park in the car park in the Farnley Hall grounds just off Hall Lane (GR 247 324).

With your back to Hall Lane and the large expanse of grass in front of you follow the broad path along the lefthand side of this, by the trees. When the path forks, bear left through the middle of a wood and emerge from the Hall grounds through a large gateway. Immediately turn right through a stile with the wall to your right. When the fence on your left ends you enter a field: bear half-left diagonally across this on a clear path. The path is joined by another one from the right and bears left. At the far side of the field pass the righthand end of a length of wall and keep forward on a paved path across the middle of the next field. Pass through a stile by a gate and walk forward; another short stretch of paved path leads to a bollard. Bear slightly right over the cross track to pass between two garages and along a narrow ginnel. Bear right along the next road for a few yards to a path signposted on the right to Fulneck. When the track reaches gates, keep forward through a stile along a narrow hedged path to another stile. A clear path leads forward to the main road.

Cross straight over to the signposted path opposite and walk down the lefthand edge of the field to cross the beck and stile in the bottom corner, then re-cross the beck and follow the clear path downhill through the woods. When you reach a clear cross path turn left along it, but in a few yards go right through a stile and down some steps. The path leads down to Tong Beck and Cockers Dale: cross the beck by the footbridge and walk forward up the slope. (You have now joined the Leeds Country Way.) Soon the path bears left and crosses a stile: keep along the bottom edge of the field with trees to your left. After some time the clear path leads through a pair of old gateposts: keep on the main path, shortly ignoring a path forking right uphill. Cross a stile and a water channel across the path coming from a small waterfall on the right (at this point there is a wide sleeper bridge on the left): keep forward on the broad path with the beck down on the left.

Just before the track begins to curve right uphill, fork left off it on a narrower path to a stile. Ignore a footbridge on the left at this point. The next stile is a few yards from the beck and the path keeps quite close to the beck. When you reach a stile by a gate, cross it and (leaving the Leeds Country Way) bear right up the track. This is Springfield Lane, which leads to Tong village. Again there are the remains of old paving, and for a while the track narrows to a footpath. At the main road, Tong Lane, cross over and turn left towards the village, but after 250 yards turn right along Keeper Lane (signposted as a bridleway to Fulneck). At a large white house at the top of the hill the track bears left through a gateway and the tarmac ends. Soon there is a view left to Tong Hall, built in 1702 and unusually for this area in brick, and forward over the valley of Pudsey Beck to Fulneck and Pudsey, and further right to Leeds.

Follow Keeper Lane down to the beck, cross the footbridge and bear right along the righthand edge of Fulneck golf course. (Now you are back on the Leeds Country Way.) At the end of the golf course cross the stile and continue along the beckside path. The clear path, never far from the beck, crosses a number of stiles and leads to the next main road, Roker Lane. Turn right downhill, and at the T-junction go left along Tong Road (leaving the Leeds Country Way for the last time). Ignore a signposted path on the right, but just over 100 yards further on, 10 yards beyond a large metal gate, there is an unsignposted stile on the right. Walk up with the hedge to your left and then on up some steps to the next stile and the motor road. Cross straight over to the stile opposite and follow the clear path up the slope. When you reach the Farnley Hall wall at the top turn left, keeping the wall to your right, along another paved path. The view left to Pudsey is impressive. Cross a stile and keep forward by the wall. Eventually you pass through a stile and join the tarmac Green Lane, which you follow back to Hall Lane, where you bear right to return to the starting point.

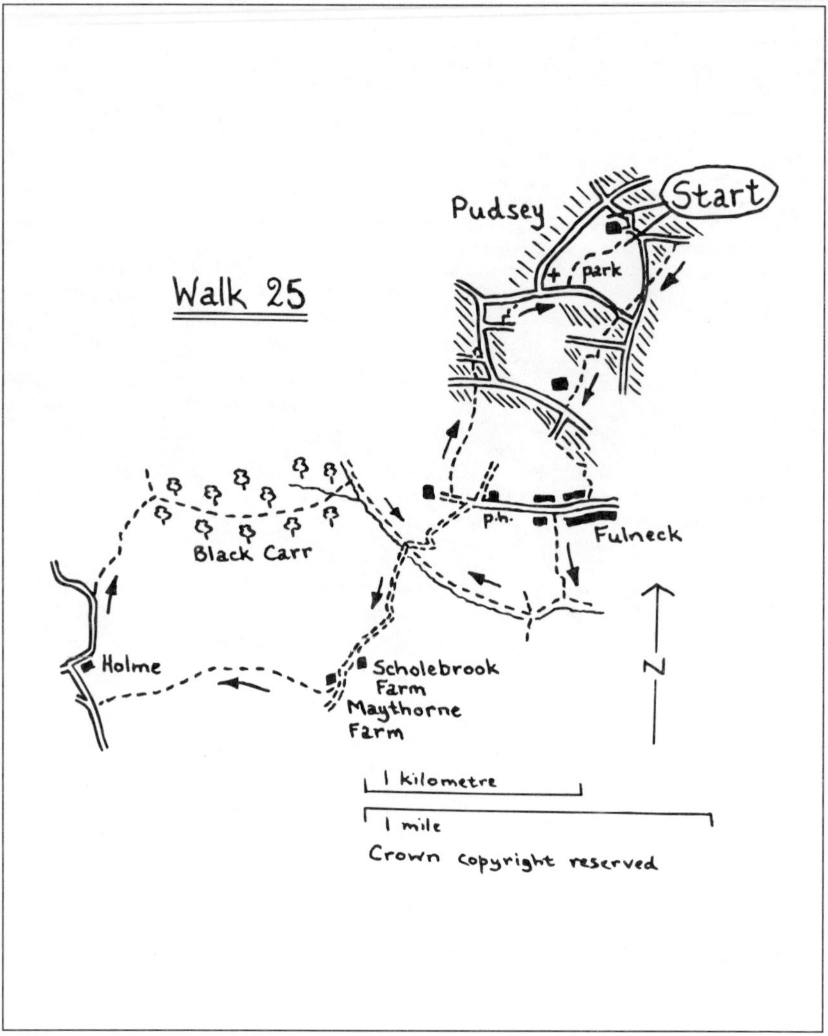

PUDSEY, FULNECK, HOLME VILLAGE AND BLACK CARR WOODS

WALK 25

5½ miles (9 km); Pathfinder 683 (SE23/33), 682 (SE03/13); a walk of great variety, good views, fine architecture, woodland and beckside paths, and horses, horses, horses.

By bus: No.4, 5, 14, 40 from the Mayfair Bingo behind Leeds Central Bus Station to Pudsey Bus Station. Walk through the car park behind the bus station and pass to the left of Pudsey Leisure Centre, keeping forward to the next main road.
By car: Park in the centre of Pudsey behind the Swimming Baths and Leisure Centre (GR 223 333). On the opposite side of the car park from the children's playground you will see a long high redbrick wall; make your way over to it and turn left alongside it, passing to the right of the Leisure Centre, and turning right at the T-junction down Crawshaw Hill to the main road.

Cross the main road and bear right, but take the first street on the left, Robin Chase, a no through road with modern houses. At the bottom, between numbers 29 and 31, keep forward for a few yards to a lamppost where you turn right along a path with chippings onto the old railway line. Keep forward along this between trees; the cutting is a superb spot for blackberries in season; it can also be muddy after rain.

When you reach the end of this section, bear right for a few yards and cross the main road, keeping the bridge to your right, to find a stile and the continuation of the path along the track of the railway. Pass through another stile and cross straight over the road, again keeping the bridge on your right, to another stile and the continuation of the path. Pass through another stile, cross over the end of the tarmac road, this time with the railway bridge to your left, to another stile and a clear path bearing right alongside the old track. The next stile brings you out onto a tarmac ginnel: turn left for a few yards to the road, then go left over the railway bridge. In 50 yards you will see a signposted public footpath on the right, a paved path. Follow it past a football pitch to the former Asda car park, across which the route of the path is marked by kerbstones. Pass through the bollards and reach the next main road by the side of the Regent pub.

Cross straight over and walk up Hillthorpe Road. At the top of the hill, in front of the house called Hillthorpe, turn left along a track, but at the gates of Fairmont fork left off the track along a ginnel. Cross straight over the next track and continue along the ginnel. At the next street turn right for a few yards, then left along a broad track, which soon bears right and soon over the wall on your left you have the first of the many fine views encountered on this ramble: over Pudsey Beck to Tong, then further left over Cockers Dale and Troy Dale. Pass between bollards and descend to the 18th century Moravian settlement of Fulneck, a haven of peace and worth exploring.

Turn right along the split-level road, but where the railing on the left ends turn left down towards a small car park. Pass to the left of this on a road bearing right downhill, but just before you reach the corner of the modern redbrick building ahead, find a set of steps forking left downhill on a paved path, soon with Fulneck Golf Club on both sides. On the way down the path makes a slight bend to the left. Keep on down, and with the golf course immediately ahead walk straight down across it (care!), keeping well to the left of a solitary tree, to Pudsey Beck, turning right alongside the beck.

When you reach a footbridge over the beck, ignore it and bear right to cross straight over a track, which also crosses the beck by a bridge, and pass through a gap-stile along a path with the beck to your left and the golf course now on the other side of the beck. The next gap-stile leads to a clear path across open pasture with the beck now some way off on the left. Cross the next stile, turn left over the footbridge and keep forward up the track (Scholebrook Lane); as you gain height notice Tong Hall over to the left. Enter the yard of Schole Brook Farm and pass to the right of the farmhouse to proceed down the tarmac access road. Immediately after passing the garden of the creeper-covered Maythorne Farm on the right, cross the stile in the wall on the right and walk forward with the farm to your right to a stile in the facing fence.

Now bear left along the old railway track, but immediately after crossing the stile by the first gate bear right off it on a clear descending path. The path keeps along close to the valley bottom through uncultivated ground with a large slag heap to the left, now much used for practice by trail riders. Soon you have a hedge to your right. On the bend where the dirt track used by the motorcyclists bears left over the beck then climbs steeply up the other side, look out for a narrow path forking right which leads along a few yards to the right of the beck. When you are faced by a fence turn left and cross the beck by a footbridge, then bear right to a stile into woodland. The path leads forward, climbing gently with the beck down to your right, until you are faced by a fence, with a gap-stile on the left. Cross this and keep straight forward uphill, keeping to the right of the old hedge, until you see a large gate in the fence ahead. A few yards to the left of this there is a stile: cross it and keep close to the lefthand edge of the field to the next stile in the far corner which leads to a narrow ginnel and the motor road at Holme.

Turn right along the road: there is an old paved footway. Drop quite steeply to Holme village and bear right past two attractive old cottages. The road climbs again: near the top, just before it bears left, cross a stile in the fence on the right and follow the wall on your right along to another stile. Now walk forward, aiming well to the left of a gate and keeping about 5 yards from the old hedge on the left, and when you reach the brow of the hill keep forward towards the fence ahead, bearing left along it to the next stile beside a large hawthorn. There are extensive views to the right. From the stile walk forward to join a cross track and turn right along this. When the track forks, keep left towards a gateway and Black Carr Woods. Follow the main track through the woods, ignoring minor paths forking left and right, until you begin to drop more steeply with a fence to your left. The track leads down to a beck, which you cross by a bridge, then keep forward over a cross track to cross a footbridge over Pudsey Beck.

Bear right with the beck to your right, and keeping always as close to the beck as you can (there are several forks) you will reach a stile a few yards to the left of the bridge you crossed on the outward route. This time turn left up the track to Bankhouse; again there are the remains of the old paving. Enjoy more fine views over the valley to Tong. A few yards before the Bankhouse Inn turn left along a stony track with the pub car park to your right. Soon you will see and follow a public footpath sign pointing over a stile by a gate on the right. Follow the track uphill to another signpost, where you bear right, keeping straight uphill on a clear narrow path. The views are superb, on a clear day the radio masts on Ilkley Moor being visible. Pass through a gap-stile and continue up the narrow ginnel. From the highest point there is a magnificent view over Leeds.

Descend the ginnel, cross over the first street and keep on along the ginnel opposite. Cross the next street and continue ahead along Smalewell Close: the footpath leads forward and then bears right to reach a main road. Turn left here, but go right into School Street. When the tarmac ends keep forward past Pudsey United Reformed church, and immediately before the tarmac begins again turn left along a narrow footpath, which soon turns right along the back of a terrace of houses. Watch out for a chance to turn left and walk along the side of the Golden Lion car park to the pub itself, where you bear right then left to reach the main road.

Turn right along the road, pass to the left of Pudsey War Memorial, and where the main road turns left at the parish church keep straight ahead down Radcliffe Lane. A few yards after the end of the church grounds go through a gate on the left into the park. Cross straight over the first cross path and walk through the attractive park, passing between gardens on the left and the bowling-green on the right, to leave the park in the far corner. Pass diagonally through the children's playground to return to the car park or bear left back to the bus station.

CALVERLEY CIRCULAR

WALK 26

5 miles (8 km); Pathfinder 683 (SE23/33), 682 (SE03/13). Easy walking on old tracks and footpaths through pleasant pastoral and wooded countryside, partly on the Leeds Country Way.

By bus: No. 670 Bradford bus from Leeds Central Bus Station to Victoria Street, Calverley (half-hourly; no service in evenings or on Sundays).
By car: In the centre of Calverley is Victoria Park with the war memorial, playing fields, bowling greens and a children's playground; at one corner is the large Methodist church. Park in Victoria Street, which runs along the opposite side of the park from the main road.

Walk along Victoria Street with the park on your left, cross over Chapel Street and pass Parkside School; cross over Thornhill Street into Rushton Street and ignore the next street forking left; cross straight over the next road and continue along Rushton Street; when you reach a T-junction turn right, then turn left at the next crossroads. In a few yards ignore a footpath sign pointing left, but at the end of the road take the signposted bridleway (Shell Lane) on the right. Now you have left the built up area.

Soon a fine view opens up left over the Aire valley towards Leeds. After some time the path bears right and climbs to a cross track: go straight over into the signposted bridleway opposite. This path soon bears left and reaches another cross track. Turn right along it. This is Priesthorpe Lane, which you follow all the way to the Leeds Ring Road, passing at one stage a golf course and later Priesthorpe School. At the ring road bear right to the large roundabout and there again go right towards Bradford; this section is noisy and smelly and boring, but it doesn't last long. At the next roundabout cross straight over Woodhall Lane, the Pudsey to Calverley road, and continue in the direction of Bradford. About 40 yards after passing the barracks, 5 yards after passing underneath a road sign, turn right between bollards (here you join the Leeds Country Way) and walk along the righthand side of the grassy area, keeping straight forward as far as you can go to find a stile, which leads left along a fenced footpath with playing fields now also to the right.

Keep with the fence when it bears right, and when you see a very clear path a yard or two to your left, join it and bear right along it through pleasant woodland. Immediately after passing through a gap in a facing fence fork left to a gap-stile, then follow the clear path straight across the field to a gap in the far wall and keep forward. Pass through a gateway and bear slightly right (a sign indicates that you are on the Leeds Country Way) to another stile, then follow the wall on your left with the golf course beyond. Pass through another stile onto the golf course. Your way now lies straight forward, over a number of fairways, where you should keep a look out for flying missiles, eventually to pass through another stile by a gate into a walled lane.

In 30 yards ignore a stile by a gate on the left, but a few yards further on keep left at a fork down a fenced track with a large deep quarry to the left. Cross a stile and keep on down the fenced path to reach another stile and a broad walled track. Turn left down this. Look out for an old stile on the right (roughly opposite the bottom of the quarry) leading onto a clear descending path under two sets of power lines. In a few yards from the stile keep right at a fork and descend the broad path to a cross track. Turn right along this and ignoring all paths and tracks forking left and right follow the main track down the valley (Carr Beck is down to your left) until shortly after you are joined by a wall on the left you pass a large mill and go through a stile by a gate onto a road. Keep forward for 25 yards, passing the entrance to the mill, then take the signposted ginnel on the left. Cross the beck by a footbridge and bear right along the track. Pass a charming corner with some stone built cottages and keep on up the lane, cobbled for a short stretch.

Cross straight over the main road at Greengates and go through the gap in the wall to the right of Carr Bottom Road. The path drops steeply by steps and soon reaches the beck side. Follow this delightful woodland path by the beck until it bears right uphill along the edge of the wood with a wall to the left. When you reach a broad track go left along it, keeping left when it forks to cross a stile by a gate and bear left down the tarmac lane. But only for a few yards, because before you reach the bridge over the Leeds and Liverpool

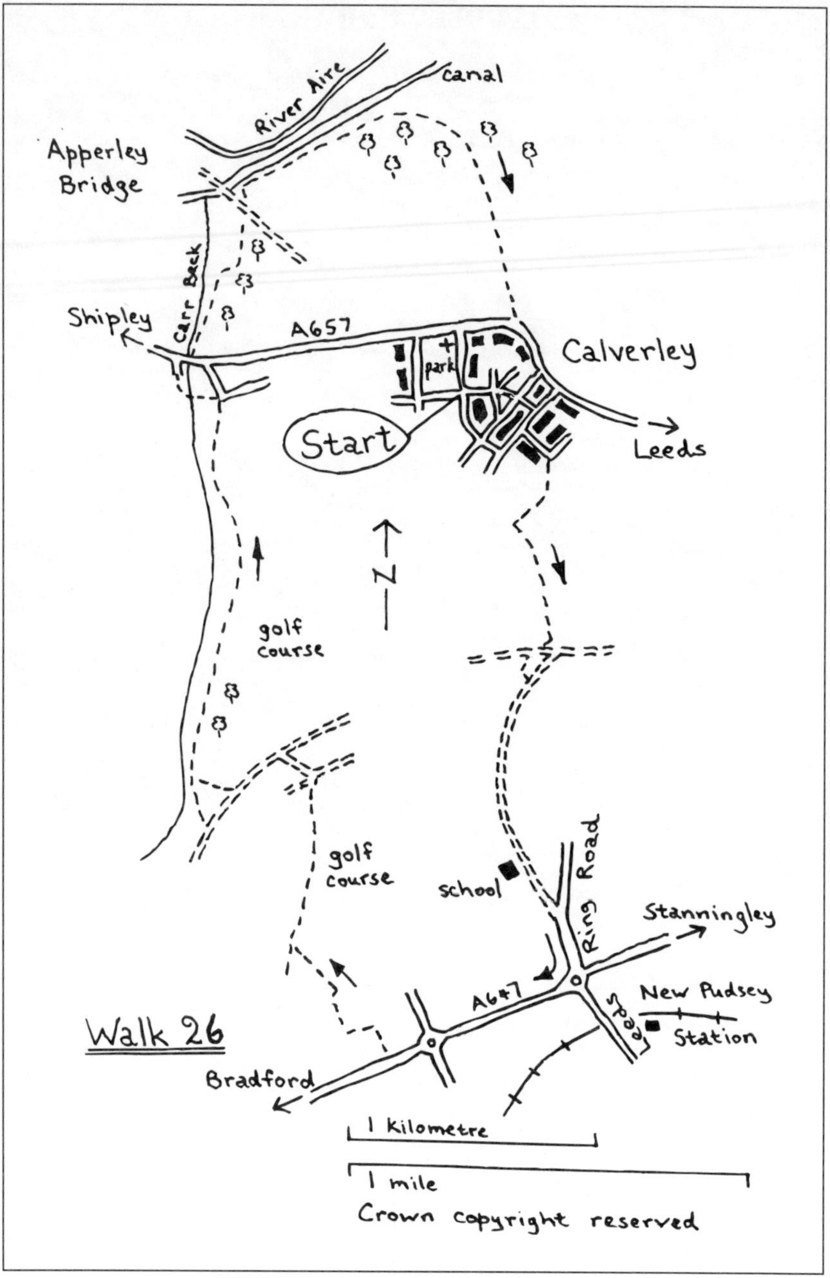

canal
River Aire
Apperley
Bridge
Carr Beck
Shipley
A657
Calverley
park
Start
Leeds
N
golf
course
golf
course
school
Ring Road
Stanningley
A647
New Pudsey
Station
Leeds
Walk 26
Bradford
1 kilometre
1 mile
Crown copyright reserved

Canal you must fork right down a track (here leaving the Leeds Country Way) which bears left to a small marina. Just before you reach the canal turn right (between two farm buildings) through a stile by a gate, then in a few yards cross another stile and keep forward with a high fence and the canal to your left.

Follow the clear track forward: it soon starts to drop towards the canal, but before it reaches it you must cross a step-stile on the right and walk along with a fence to your left and the wood to your right. Soon the path is a few yards inside the wood, parallel to the canal. Shortly after passing under a pylon the path bears right away from the canal, but still close to the edge of the wood. Shortly after the path begins to climb gently, look out for a path forking left to a stile in the wall on the left. Cross this and keep right along the top side of the field. There is a fine view across the canal to Cragg Wood and Rawdon. Soon another stile takes you back into the wood. Rejoin the path you were on earlier, go left, but immediately keep right at a fork on an ascending path away from the edge of the wood. For a short distance you have a high wall to the right.

Now it is easy to get lost. Pass an old gatepost. A track comes in from the right: bear left for a few yards, then fork left off this track, but then immediately right again (in spite of the yellow arrow!) on a narrow ascending path with the track you have just left down below you on the right. Keep along the edge, with the drop to your right, then bear slightly left with the path to reach the lefthand edge of the wood; keep uphill on a clear path with the wall and fields to the left. About 40 yards after reaching the edge of the wood find a stile in the wall on the left, cross it and bear right up the outside edge of the wood. Now your problems of route-finding are over.

The clear path leads round to a cottage, with a stile on the left immediately in front of it. Keep down the field with the wood to your right. The tower of Calverley Parish Church is visible ahead. Go through a gated stile beside a large gate and keep forward with a playing field to the left, then Calverley School, to reach the main road. Bear right along it, and when you are opposite the Methodist church cross the road and go up Chapel Street to the left of the church. Soon there is access to the children's playground and the park. There is an exit from the top side of the park onto Victoria Street.

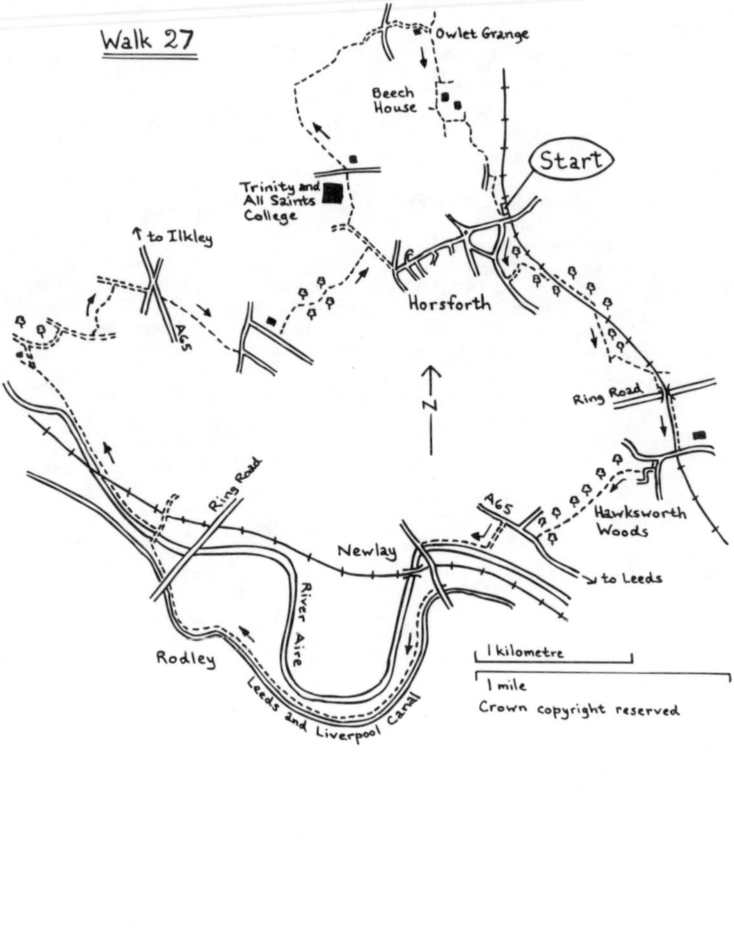
Walk 27
Owlet Grange
Beech House
Start
Trinity and All Saints College
to Ilkley
A65
Horsforth
N
Ring Road
Hawksworth Woods
A65
to Leeds
Ring Road
Newlay
River Aire
Rodley
Leeds and Liverpool Canal
1 kilometre
1 mile
Crown copyright reserved

HORSFORTH CIRCULAR

WALK 27

9 miles (14.5 km); Pathfinder 683 (SE23/33), 672 (SE 24/34); a most attractive and varied walk, using woodland paths in the NW Leeds built-up area, canal and riverside paths, and field paths with distant views; the only drawback is that several busy roads have to be crossed.

By train: Leeds to Horsforth (Harrogate Line).
By car: Park in the car park at Horsforth Station (GR 244 391).

Return to the main road (Station Road) and cross straight over to walk down Troy Road. Pass the Low Lane Car Centre and 50 yards further on turn left down the tarmac drive to the Brookfoot Estate, keeping by the wall/fence to your right until you join a footpath to the right of a large factory building. Cross the beck and keep straight forward through the wood, turning right along an old cobbled cross path with a wall to the left. With the railway close by on the left, just past an open space look out for a path forking left through an old stile into a walled ginnel with the railway immediately to the left. Where it ends go left under the railway, then immediately turn right off the tarmac path onto a clear path which in a few yards joins a broad path forward through the woods.

This path in turn joins another tarmac footpath along which you bear right, but in 80 yards fork right off it on a broad path down into the woods. Ignore minor paths forking left and right, and your path will bear right to pass under the railway again. Bear left on the broad woodland path, which passes to the right of the noisy Tweed House boarding kennels. A few yards before you reach the bridge over the beck turn sharp left uphill, still to the right of the kennels, then bear right on an ascending path back into the woods. The path soon for a short distance follows the edge of the wood with fields on the right. About 20 yards before the track leads under the railway again fork right off it on a clear path which soon has a wall to the left and fields to the right. Follow this to the Leeds Ring Road.

Cross the Ring Road with great care and turn left, passing under the railway yet again, then immediately turn right on the signposted path on grass, with the fence, wood and railway to the right, and enter the woods on a narrow ascending path up Butcher Hill. Soon you are higher than the railway, with Abbey Grange School to your left. At the main road turn right, crossing the railway for the last time. Ignore a road forking left, but 50 yards further on take a ginnel on the left, which leads to Cragside Close, where you bear right. The street soon bears left, and there is a stile in the fence on the right into Hawksworth Woods. In a few yards keep left at a fork, and when you reach a clear cross path bear left along it with a valley to your right. Ignore paths forking right or left and eventually you will be led down to the A65 opposite Gate 2 into Kirkstall Forge.

Again you have a busy road to cross with great care, then turn right along it. A sign soon tells you that you are entering Horsforth once more. Immediately after the first house on the left turn left down a stony track (bridleway sign). Cross the old Kirkstall Forge Goit just before the track bears right, and now you are close to the river Aire. When you reach a stile by a gate you can hear and glimpse the weir on the left at which the mill race starts. Walk forward and then turn left over the cobbled Newlay Bridge, erected in 1819 and one of the oldest iron bridges in the county. This is a delightful spot. Now you enter the Kirkstall Valley Park. Keep forward along the road, cross the modern railway bridge (Leeds to Ilkley/Skipton lines) – down on the right is the 18th century Abbey Inn – and follow the road towards the bridge over the Leeds and Liverpool Canal, but a few yards before the bridge fork left onto the towpath and turn right along it, passing under the bridge.

Follow the towpath all the way to Rodley. If you want to visit the Rodley Barge, with its canalside terrace, you will have to walk on to the next swing bridge after the pub, cross it and then return on the other side, but our walk continues along the towpath to pass under the Leeds Ring Road. Ignore an access road coming in from the right, but a short distance further on fork right off the towpath along a stony track past the Railway Inn.

Ignore a cobbled track forking left and follow your track right to the cobbled bridge over the Aire. A few yards beyond the bridge cross the stile in the fence on the left, soon to pass under a pylon and follow the direction of the power lines. Now for some distance we shall be close to the river. Cross a stile and pass under two railway bridges, then continue along the riverside path, which can be very overgrown in summer.

Cross a footbridge and follow the path to a stile where a fence meets a wall, after which the path bears right away from the river to reach in a few yards a T-junction with fields in front. Go left here, soon with a wall to your left. When you reach a modern house, pass to the right of it up the access road (here joining the Leeds Country Way). When you meet a cross track go right, and at the next T-junction again go right, once more on tarmac. At a junction of several roads and tracks bear sharp left up a narrow path between hedges, soon passing through a barrier. This old walled path is a fine place for blackberries in season. Shortly after passing through another barrier turn right along a stony track, and at the first tarmac road turn left up to the A65 again.

Turn right and you will already see a footpath sign on the other side of the road 100 yards ahead. Cross the road again with great care and go through the gap in the wall by the sign and down the steps into the field. The path leads across the corner of the field to a stile into the woods. Cross Gill Beck by the footbridge and climb steeply up some steps and into a hedged ginnel. Where this ends go through the gap-stile and keep forward with the remains of a hedge to your left. There is a splendid view over Airedale. The path may not always be clear, but keep forward and at the far end of the field bear right still with the hedge to your left. Follow the hedge round to a stile, cross it and follow the hedge on your left to another stile and then to another stile by a gate. Keep forward, soon between hedges, to another stile into a ginnel.

At the road turn left, then left again at the T-junction, then take the first road on the right (West End Lane). Immediately past West End School go through the stile on the left into woodland. When you reach a fork with a couple of sleepers on the ground and the main path going straight ahead uphill, fork right onto a narrower path, also uphill. You are joined by a path from the left and immediately after that there is a fork: keep right along the main path (there is a yellow arrow on a wooden pylon); you are joined by another path from the left and soon reach a glade with a junction of several paths: look left to find a yellow waymark on a tree and turn sharp left uphill past this tree, and when you reach a broader path bear right up it, soon with a wall to the left, on the top edge of the wood. Keep on the main path over Hunger Hills and leave the wood over a stile, to walk along the edge of the field with the hedge to your left. The view over Leeds is excellent.

Go through the stile by the gate onto Lee Lane. Turning right here and then bearing left at the bottom would be a short cut back to Horsforth Station, but our route turns left along with the wall to our left. A few yards before the tarmac road at Lee Lane Farm turn sharp right (footpath sign) on a rather indistinct path, which follows a fence on the left down towards the running track in the grounds of Trinity and All Saints College. Bear left along a paved path, which is almost immediately joined by another paved path from the right, but where the paved path goes through a gate bear right along a hedged path, with the college buildings to the left, and follow it to Brownberrie Lane.

Cross the road into the drive to Brownberrie House, but in a yard or two go through the stile in the wall on the left and follow the clear path through the wood. Go through a kissing-gate and ignore the path forking right along the fence. On emerging from the wood immediately bear left to a stile into a field, which you cross diagonally right to another stile. Bear right along the edge of the next field with a wood to your right. At the end of the wood ignore the gate ahead and keep forward with the hedge to your right, pass through a gap in a cross hedge and follow the hedge on your right until you reach a stile in it. Cross this and walk down the field to a stile in the far lefthand corner. Keep forward with the wall on your left, cross another stile and cut the corner of the next field by walking along the row of airport approach lights, to return to the wall on your left. Keep with the wall until your only exit is over a stile in it. Bear right down the tarmac lane.

At the foot cross straight over Scotland Lane and bear left down the farm access road opposite. Pass to the left of Owlet Grange and immediately after it fork right (footpath sign). At the end of the track cross the step-stile (now redundant) in the wall on the left and walk forward a few yards to another stile. Here we part company with the Leeds Country Way, which turns left, for we go right along the edge of the field with a wall to our right. At the end of the field cross the stile and walk forward with a hedge to the right. At the far end of this field, with a wood ahead, cross a stile onto a track: ignore the first track to the right, walk forward a couple of yards and take the second track to the right, which soon bears left with a wall to the left.

Pass the entrance to Beech House on the left and keep forward along the track (footpath sign). At the end of the wood on the left leave the track by crossing a stile on the left and walk down the lefthand edge of the field. When you reach a gate on the left with a stile beside it, bear threequarters right across the field to a stile in the wall on the far side. Cross the broken sleeper bridge beyond and keep forward with the fence to your left to another stile in the wall ahead. Over this bear half left down the next field to a stile a yard or two up from the far corner. Walk straight across the next field to the next stile, then forward along the street for about 50 yards to find a ginnel on the left between the houses. At the bottom of this bear right along the track to return to Horsforth Station.

RAWDON BILLING AND CRAGG WOOD

WALK 28

5 miles (8 km); Pathfinder 683 (SE 23/33); airy views, woodland and riverside; some paths, including the one by the river, can be overgrown in summer.

By bus: No. 732, 733, 734, 735, 736 Otley/Ilkley bus from Leeds Central Bus Station to Rawdon cross-roads.
By car: Park in the car park by the library and council offices at the top end of Micklefield Park, on the A65 Leeds to Ilkley road a few yards on the Guiseley side of the junction with the A658 Bradford to Harrogate road (GR 208 397).

Return to the traffic lights and walk along the Harrogate Road on the righthand side of the road. About 70 yards from the lights turn into a signposted ginnel on the right in the middle of a terrace of shops and climb the steps up Pease Hill. On the way up you cross over one street and at the top you cross another, continuing forward along the pavement. Cross yet another street and keep forward along Peasehill Park to re-enter the ginnel, which you follow to the next main road, crossing a tarmac drive on the way. Cross the main road and turn right along the pavement. At the T-junction bear left past the Emmott Arms, then take the first street on the left (Billing View).

Follow the tarmac up, ignoring Billing Court on the right, and bear right at the top, pass a public footpath signpost and fork left along a track just before a terrace of houses (still Billing View). At the end of the houses keep forward along the track with a small reservoir to the right. The track soon narrows to a footpath between hedges (a fine place for blackberries in season), and when it opens out again by some upright posts, fork left uphill towards the wood. When you reach a cross path turn left up it and follow it round to a stile. On your right is the reclaimed quarry of Rawdon Billing, which you may like to explore, and extensive views open up to the left. Cross the stile and walk forward along the edge of the bank on a clear path, before bearing slightly right in the direction of the trig point. But when you reach a fence corner by a hawthorn bush on the left, well before the trig point, turn sharp right and walk down the field with a hedge to your left. When the hedge ends keep on by the wall, bearing right with it at the bottom of the field to pass through a gate in the far corner. Bear left downhill parallel to the hedge/wall on your left. Pass to the left of the reservoir to reach a stile onto the playing fields at Rawdon School and walk forward behind the goalposts to reach a tarmac path which passes to the left of the wall enclosing the school playground. The path bears right, drops down a few steps, then turns left to reach Town Street, Rawdon.

Cross Town Street and turn left, but take the first road on the right (Carr Lane). About halfway down, by a lamppost, go right along a signposted ginnel, which leads you down to the A65. Cross this busy road with care and take the farm access track to Rawdon Carrs opposite. Go through the large gate into the farmyard then immediately cross a gap-stile on the right. Walk straight across the field to another gap-stile in the wall opposite, then half-left down the next field to a stile to the left of a gate. Now bear slightly right down to the next stile some 10 yards to the right of the trees in the bottom of the field, then keep the same line down to another stile into a narrow strip of woodland. Bear slightly right through this to another stile, then walk straight down the next large field, passing to the left of a low embankment, to a stile by a gate.

Cross over the tarmac road into a walled ginnel opposite. At the end of this keep forward for a few yards with the wall to your right, but where this ends bear left in front of the holly bushes on a rather rough path with a high bank to the left, before bearing right again on a track down into the wood with an overgrown wall to your left. This area, sloping down to the river Aire, is known as Cragg Wood. Pass round a gate and cross a stony track, to descend the tarmac lane opposite. Pass to the left of a modern house then fork right, down towards a metal gate, but before you reach it turn right down a fenced path to a kissing-gate, then keep forward between a fence on the left and the wood on the right. Parts of this path can be overgrown in summer. Soon you are close to the Aire.

Follow the riverside path until, shortly before the river is spanned by a railway bridge, you cross a stile into playing fields. Turn right along the wall on your right, and at the rough grass the path bears left (through the rough grass!) to cut the corner and continue with the wall/fence to your right and soon with a line of trees to your left. When the trees end keep forward to cross a stile by a gate on the right and a few yards further on you join a motor road. Turn right along it. When the road bears right, keep forward up a tarmac drive (bridleway sign on the lamppost), and at the next cottage bear right into a walled lane. Soon it bears left and you ascend between high walls.

When you reach a junction of several drives, keep straight forward uphill in the broad walled lane. Look out for a narrow walled ginnel forking left off it and follow this up to a tarmac drive. Cross over this and continue up the ginnel. When you reach the next broad track turn right along it; it leads across the middle of Rawdon Golf Course (caution!), bearing left to reach a tarmac road beside the golf club car park. Turn right up to the main road, and right again there. Soon there is a gate on the left into the park, which you can explore before returning to the starting point.

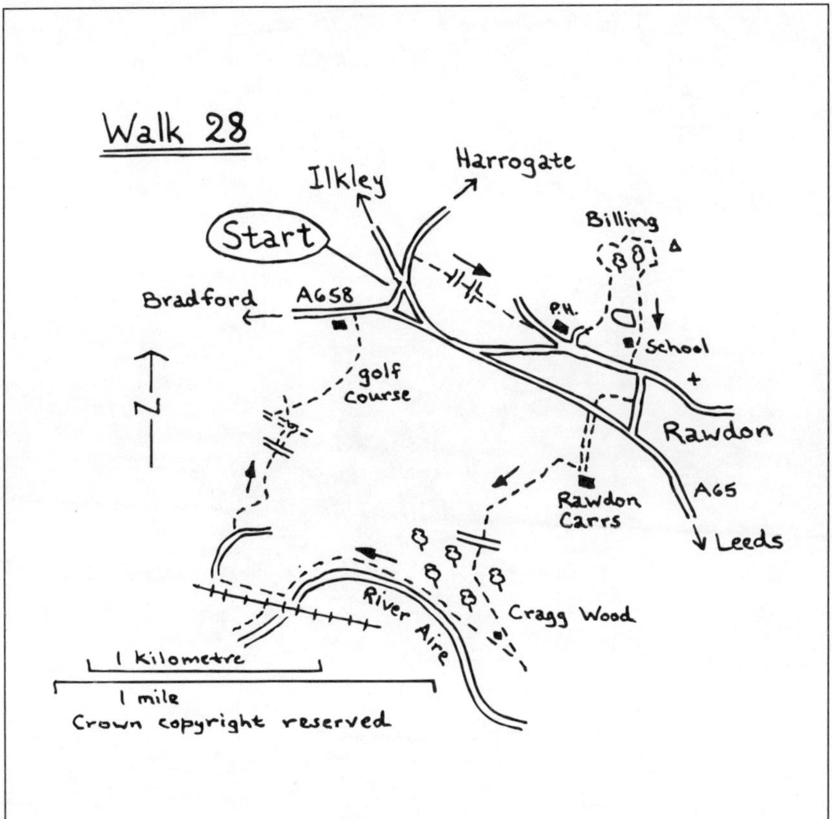

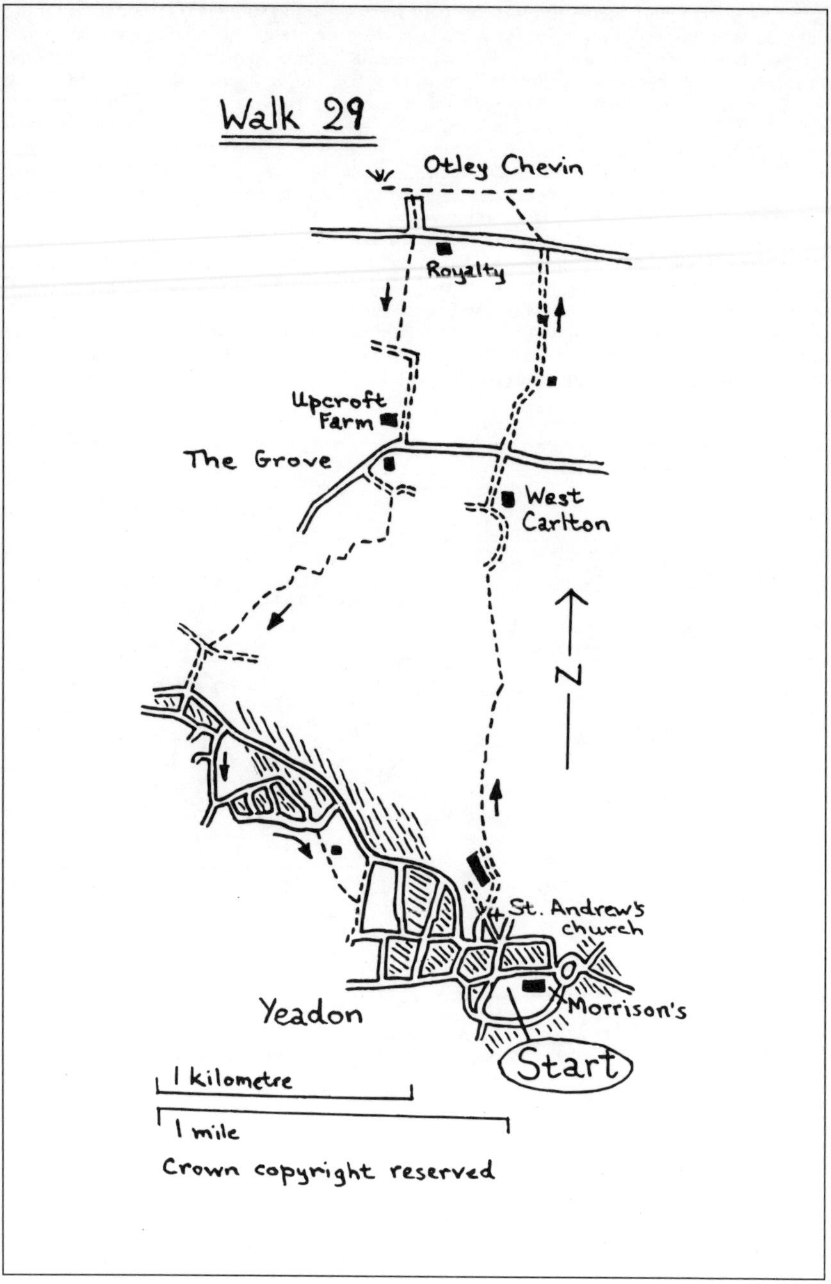
Walk 29
Otley Chevin
Royalty
Upcroft Farm
The Grove
West Carlton
N
St. Andrew's church
Morrison's
Yeadon
Start
1 kilometre
1 mile
Crown copyright reserved

YEADON TO OTLEY CHEVIN

WALK 29

5 miles (8 km); Pathfinder 672 (SE24/34), 671 (SE04/14); an easy stroll to the ridge between Airedale and Wharfedale, with fine views on both sides.

By bus: No.655, 755, 731, 735, 736 from Leeds Central Bus Station to Yeadon Town Hall. Note that the return bus to Leeds does not leave from the High Street, which is one-way, but from Harper Lane, which is the road on the top side of Morrison's.
By car: Park in one of the car parks in the centre of Yeadon: there is space around the Town Hall, or drive down to the foot of High Street and either turn left, where there is a car park after 100 yards on the right, or turn right to find another one after 100 yards on the right. Note that the large Morrison's car park is private, with a two hour limit.

Make your way to the bottom of the High Street, there turning right past the NatWest bank. Take the stony track to the left of St.Andrew's church along the front of a terrace of cottages (North Terrace), then keep downhill to the next road junction and bear right (bridleway sign) along the tarmac drive to the right of the Scott & Rhodes factory. In 60 yards do not go through the large blue gates into the works but turn right through the bollards and then immediately left with the factory wall to your left. A gate leads into open country. Pass a gate on the left into the works and keep forward still with the wall to your left.

Cross a stile by a gate ahead and keep forward, now with gardens on the left and a fence on the right. Ignore stiles in this fence. When the gardens end pass through the kissing-gate into the field and walk straight across it to the next gate. On the horizon, slightly to the left of the wood, can be seen the Royalty pub, which you may want to visit later on the walk. The next gate is an interesting combination of gate and stile: from it keep straight forward to the next gate, then on for a short distance with a wall to the left, but where that bears left keep forward down the field on a clear path to cross a wooden footbridge and a stile into a fenced path.

At the end of this pass through a gap-stile and continue with a wall to your right. Cross a stile by a gate and keep on along the track, still with the wall to your right. Bear right with the wall and cross another stile by a gate to enter a walled lane, which leads to West Carlton Farm. Here walk straight forward up the tarmac access road to the next motor road, cross it diagonally right and continue along the stony walled lane. Pass to the left of a bungalow and follow the lane up to the next motor road. Ignore the gate and stile opposite and go left for 15 yards to a gap-stile in the wall on the right, which is immediately followed by a wooden stile, and follow the clear path half-left through the young plantation. Now an extensive view opens up over Wharfedale and beyond. Cross a stile in a fence and continue on the same line to the next (redundant) stile just to the left of two old stone gateposts.

At the cross track go left (going straight ahead would take you down to Otley), enjoying increasingly fine views. Notice a stile on the left into a car park with a notice board and map of the Chevin Forest Park, which will be our return route, but meanwhile spend as much time exploring this part of the Chevin as you feel like. Then cross the stile and walk through the car park. The Royalty is a short distance to the left, but our route continues through the gap-stile opposite. Follow a faint path down the field parallel to the wall on the left but some way from it – there is a good view of the main runway of the Leeds/Bradford Airport from this field – to a stile in the wall at the bottom. Continue down the next field, now with the wall to your right. Cross the stile and turn left along the walled lane. It soon bears right and descends past Upcroft Farm to the next motor road.

Turn right along this. Pass a large house called The Grove on the left and 100 yards after it turn left into a signposted stony track. After passing through a gate, the track forks: ignore a gate on the right and keep forward with the wall/fence to your left. Shortly before you reach a facing gate cross the stile on the right and walk forward along an old hedged way. This leads to a gap in a facing wall. Ignore the stile on the left here and turn right along the wall, keeping it to your right. When the wall ends keep forward to pass between two old stone gateposts and pass a redundant stile to reach a footpath sign by a facing hedge. Turn left, and keeping a ditch on your right walk down the edge of the field until you come to a wooden bridge over the ditch and a stile in the wall. Cross this and turn left to follow the edge of the field down, going right with the wall at the bottom to reach a gap-stile in the next corner. Through this bear left down the edge of the field in a fenced path. Follow this to another stile, then still keep near the lefthand edge of the field, now with no fence to your right but with a beck to your left. Pass through a gap-stile onto a lane, go left along it for a few yards, but where it bears left fork right off it through a stile and bear right down the field parallel to the wall on your right. Cross a gap-stile in the field corner and continue with the wall on your right to another stile near a gate, from which you follow the wall on your right down to another stile and the main road.

We are now back in Yeadon, and want to return to the town centre by as green as route as possible. Cross the road and take the signposted ginnel opposite, turning left along the road at the far end. Ignore the first street forking right (St Oswald's Garth), but bear right at the next T-junction down Ruskin Crescent, with playing fields to your left. Follow the road down to a T-junction with a posting box on the left and a telephone kiosk on the right and there bear left, but take the first street on the right (the name is facing away from you, but it is Tennyson Street: this is obviously the literary part of Yeadon!); it soon bends left, and you want to follow it along (passing Bacon Street and Masefield Street!) until you reach an open space on the right with swings and a 'rocket': turn right down this grassy area on a clear path, pass to the left of another football pitch, drop to cross a wooden footbridge over the beck and bear right up the steps into Nunroyd Park.

You reach a tarmac drive with the Inn on the Park to your left. Follow the sign saying Entrance to the Inn and walk past the front of the pub. Immediately after this fork right and then left over a footbridge, then right along the bank of the small lake. Do not cross the bridge at the far end, but stand with your back to the bridge and walk straight forward up the grassy slope towards a gap in a line of trees. Pass behind the goalposts at the lefthand end of the rugby pitch (Yeadon seems well provided with playing fields!) to a gateway in the fence ahead and keep forward along the grassy track to more old gateposts and a T-junction: turn right along the stony track. To your left over the wall is yet another football pitch.

Immediately before you reach the tarmac road, with Kirk Lane allotments to the right, turn left into the park (there is a ginnel just outside the park, but it is more pleasant inside); here there are more swings if required, but the walk continues along the righthand edge of the park to leave it in the far corner, where you do have to turn left along the ginnel. Turn right at the T-junction. The street almost immediately bears left; ignore a footpath sign on the right and keep forward to the next T-junction at Swincar Avenue: cross straight over and continue up the dirt track with a factory on your right. Bear left round a new extension to the factory and continue up the fenced path. At the next T-junction bear right for a few yards, then at the next junction bear left uphill. Turn right at the top of the hill, and now you have rejoined your outward route, with the NatWest bank in front of you.

HAWKSWORTH

WALK 30

5 miles (8 km); Pathfinder 671 (SE 04/14). An easy ramble on clear paths, a mixture of pasture and woodland, with fine views.

By bus: *No. 731/732/733 Leeds to Otley/Ilkley from Leeds Central Bus Station or No. 33 Leeds to Otley from Vicar Lane to the White Cross (near Harry Ramsden's) in Guiseley. Walk along to the White Cross pub. At the roundabout cross over the Bradford Road and take the next minor road off the roundabout on the left (Thorpe Lane). There is no pavement, but walk along the righthand verge with a wood to your right. The road climbs, and on a lefthand bend a signposted bridleway leaves it on the right. Walk along this, ignore the entrance to Thorpe Farm on the right and go through the gate ahead, and a few yards further on fork left along a track to a stile by a cattle-grid. High Royds Hospital is over to your right. Follow the track to the next farm, which is derelict, cross the cattle-grid just before you reach it and then the stile by the gate to the left of the buildings. Ignore a track forking right and keep forward to the stile by the next gate. Cross it and turn sharp left up the hillside.*
By car: *drive to the west end of Hawksworth and continue along Old Lane, straight over at the crossroads and along Goose Lane to its junction with the Bingley Road; turn right here and a short way along on the right is a very large layby: park here, and start the walk description at [*].*

The faint path is parallel to the fence on the left. The pull up this gorse covered hillside is quite stiff, and you bear slightly right away from the fence, but take care not to go too far right, because your next stile is behind a gorse bush in the fence at the top. Cross and walk straight over the large field. There is a fine view back to Menston, Guiseley and the Chevin. As you come over the crest you will see the next stile in the wall ahead, with trees beyond. This leads into a fenced path which brings you to Hawksworth. Cross diagonally right over the village street and walk down a short track between houses leading down to a white gate. Cross the stile beside the gate and keep forward through the yard to another stile ahead. Over this follow the path down the field, reaching the righthand edge where the fence becomes a wall. Continue down the wall side, crossing three stiles to enter a narrow fenced path, which eventually turns right, crosses the beck by a small slab bridge and crosses another stile. Turn left downhill, now with the wall to your left, to another stile into the woods, and follow the clear path down to the valley bottom, being joined near the foot by a path from the left.

Don't cross the beck by the stepping stones, but turn right over the stile. Follow this lovely woodland path to another stile, then keep forward for a few more yards to cross the beck by more stepping stones. In a few yards the path forks: ignore the stile ahead (signposted White House) and fork right (signposted Sconce Lane). The path keeps parallel to the beck on the right for some distance before climbing away from it to a stile in the wall on the left. It is in fact a double stile, forward then right, then you bear left up the field edge with a wall to your left to another stile in the top corner. Bear left along the edge of the field, soon bearing right with the wall. When the wall ends keep along the fence to a gap-stile in the wall ahead into the garden of a house. Walk forward to pass to the right of the house and through a gate in the fence ahead. Continue through the next garden to the facing fence, where you turn left through the white gate and along a ginnel to a tarmac drive.

Bear right up to the motor road and turn right along it. Where the road bends right fork left off it up a track, and follow this until it kinks right and then left to pass through Faweather Grange. Having gone through the gate fork right downhill, and shortly fork right again off the main track onto a grassy track descending between walls. It bears right to a gate, and you cross the beck by a clapper bridge. Continue up the track, taking care not to bear right off it into the field (there is a signpost). The next section can be excessively wet, but it does not last long. There are short sections of old paving in this walled track. Pass through two gates, then to the left of houses, and follow the track to the Bingley Road. Turn right along it, ignoring the next road on the right which leads back to Hawksworth. Car drivers should find their cars in the layby a little further on.

[*] From the layby continue along the wide grass verge in the Menston direction, with Reva Reservoir to your right, and follow the road until you reach a footpath signpost pointing right over a stile by a gate and along a broad fenced track (a notice on the gate says Wharfedale Scout Sailing Centre). Follow the track, but where it bears right down to the reservoir, cross the stile straight ahead and keep forward on the grassy path with a fence to the right. Where the fence joins a wall bear left on a clear path about 15 yards left of the wall. The path keeps parallel to the wall and reaches a stile in a facing fence/wall. Cross this and bear right with the fence to your right, bearing slightly left when the fence becomes a wall, and follow this wall to another stile in a facing fence. Cross this into the grounds of stables and bear left along the fence on your left to a stile and a road.

Turn right along the road for about 50 yards to a signposted path on the left. Cross the stile, which is immediately followed by a gate, and walk along the track, vith a view left to Otley Chevin. The track passes through a gate with a stile to the left of it. For a short distance you are in the remains of an old walled lane. Follow the track as far as the next gate, about 100 yards before farm buildings. Those who came by car will not cross the stile, but will turn right up the slope and jump to the start of the walk description, those who came by bus will cross the stile and walk towards the derelict farm.

(For those returning by bus, a pleasant alternative end to the walk would be to walk down to Menston and catch the bus there. So turn left immediately before the derelict farm down to a pair of gates. Pass through and follow the track. Cross the stile by the next gate and continue on the track. The fine old house ahead is High Royds Hall. When you reach the outbuildings of the Hall, pass through the kissing-gate and keep forward down the access road. This leads to the Bingley Road in Menston. Turn right there, and at the next junction keep forward, passing a recreation ground on your left, to return to the A65 at traffic lights. The bus stop for Leeds is a few yards to your right, on the other side of the road.)

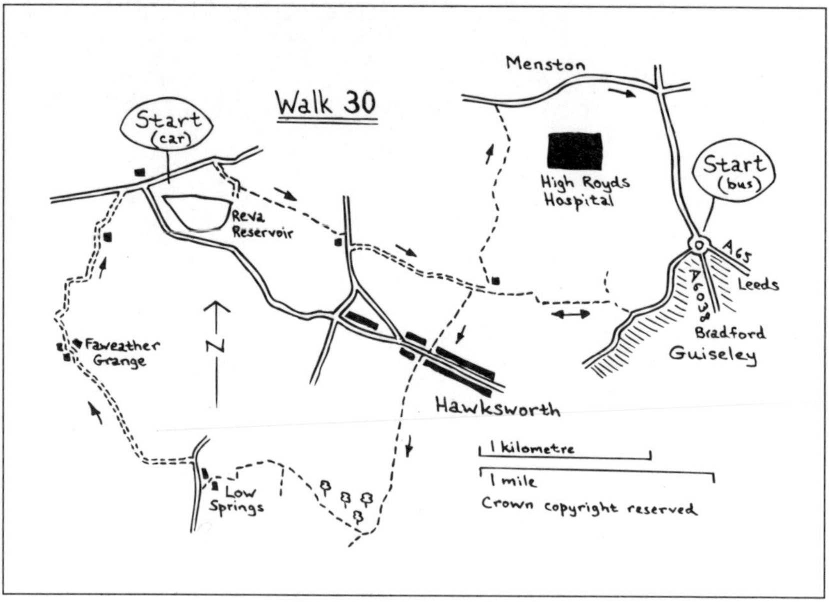

MENSTON, BURLEY AND THE WEST CHEVIN

WALK 31

6½ miles (10 km); Pathfinder No. 671 (SE 04/14); a varied ramble with fine views.

By bus: No. 731/732/733 Leeds to Otley/Ilkley via Menston from Leeds Central Bus Station to the entrance to High Royds Hospital on the A65. Walk along the main road towards Menston and at the traffic lights turn left into Bingley Road.
By car: take the A65 from Leeds to Guiseley, pass Morrisons's on the left and turn right at the traffic lights by the Station pub; cross the railway bridge and turn left into Netherfield Road; just after leaving the 30 m.p.h. limit there is a large cemetery on the left, and at the far end of this a layby on the right, just before a public bridleway sign on each side of the road. Park here and take the bridleway downhill, starting the walk description at [*] below.

Walk along Bingley Road, with a wood to your left. At the far end of a recreation ground on the right the main road turns right as Main Street and on the left is an entrance into High Royds Hospital. Keep straight forward, still on Bingley Road. Shortly after passing Cleasby Road the footway crosses the road, and at the de-restriction sign it ends. Follow the road uphill, and 50 yards after the next house on the right cross the signposted stile in the wall on the right and bear half-left up the slope to pass to the left of a wooden pylon. There is a view right over Menston and back to the Chevin.

There is another stile in the wall ahead just to the left of some trees: over it keep on with the wall/fence to your right to a stile in it about 35 yards along. Cross this and bear half-left across the next field towards the trees on the far side. Cross the stile onto the road and turn right downhill. At the end of a field on the left, just before the start of a terrace of stone houses, turn left through a stile and along a ginnel, with the field to your left. The ginnel leads to a stile into a field: continue along the righthand edge of this, looking out for where a kissing-gate leads out of the field, past the end of a terrace of houses, where you bear right over the gravel to another road. Bear right along the road.

Where the road bends right into the village, with a fine 17th-century house ahead, turn left along Bleach Mill Lane, which shortly bears left between walls. You are now on the Ebor Way and the Leeds Dales Way Link. Soon you have a view right to Burley and over the Wharfe to Askwith and the moors beyond. Shortly after passing an attractive millpond don't go through the wide gateway into Bleach Mill but fork left on the narrow path round the outside of the grounds. Light refreshments may be available at Bleach Mill. The path leads to a step-stile: cross this and bear left with a wall to your right.

A few yards after you cross Carr Beck go through a gap-stile in the wall on the right (another path comes downhill on the left by the beck) and walk straight downhill parallel to the beck on your right through attractive parkland landscape; there is a clear path. Cross the gap-stile in the bottom righthand corner of the field and keep down with the beck to your right. Cross another stile and keep straight on down the next field, losing the beck for a while. Soon you come close to the righthand edge of the field again and a small beck emerges through a pipe. Soon you cross two stiles in quick succession and keep on along the edge of the field with the beck to your right. Rejoin the main beck. Cross a stile very close to the beck and keep on beside the beck until you cross it by a footbridge of sorts, a few yards beyond which is a redundant stile.

Now you must pay attention to route-finding. Keep on in the same direction as before, bisecting the angle of the corner of the field, and crossing the field diagonally towards trees on the far side. There is no path. About 20 yards to the right of the beck you pass through the line of trees, crossing the ditch by a bridge, and bear slightly left, parallel to the beck, crossing it in about 100 yards by a sleeper bridge near a small construction of stone slabs. Cross the stile in the fence ahead at the foot of the railway embankment and bear left up this, cross the Leeds to Ilkley railway with great care and descend the embankment to a stile. A clear path now leads down the slope. Turn left at the cross-path at the bottom through woodland. Keep right at a fork and follow the path to a stile in the fence on the right, cross, walk forward a yard or two and turn left to another stile. Mount some steps onto the old Ilkley to Otley line, go left for 10 yards and fork half-right down some more broad steps and into a tarmac ginnel.

Now we must make our way through the south-eastern fringe of Burley in Wharfedale. When you reach a street go right for a few yards then fork left into the continuation of the ginnel. Pass through barriers to another street: cross over and keep on along the ginnel. You cross and re-cross the beck. At the next street walk forward a few yards to find the continuation of the tarmac footpath on the left. At the T-junction go left over the footbridge then right down the track, following the beck on your right. Ignore a private footbridge and the next public footbridge on the right, but a few yards beyond it go right over a clapper bridge and stile into a field and walk forward, keeping an old hedge to your left to a stile onto the A65.

Turn left towards Burley and at the next junction turn right along the old A660 Otley Road. After 250 yards fork half-right along a signposted track passing to the left of some modernised houses and past a sign saying Private Road: Access to Goit Stock Farm. After passing some barns the track leads past the farmhouse, a modern building, after which it becomes grassy. Follow the track to the very end, where you are faced by a stile by a gate, beyond which you cross a beck by stepping stones of sorts. Walk straight up the middle of the large field towards the wood to a stile in the fence at the top, keeping well to the right of a small stone building in the top lefthand corner of the field.

The stile leads onto Otley Golf Course, where you must beware of flying missiles! Cross half-left towards the wood, passing through some trees on the way. Make for a spot about 60 yards left of the lefthand end of the fence at the far side, marked by blue wooden posts. Here a path comes down through the wood, crossing the ditch onto the golf course by a sleeper bridge. Don't cross this, but stand with your back to it, facing out over the golf course. Walk straight back over the fairway, to a blue post a few yards to the left of some trees. Now turn right through the trees to another post 15 yards before a small stone building. Bear left past this building and across a fairway to a tall rusty metal post just to the right of some trees, then bear right to another small blue post, passing to the left of a large old stone gatepost, and now half-right to the next post a short distance before the car-park. Now follow the series of posts to the right round the car-park and left between ornamental trees to reach the access drive to the golf club. Bear right along this to the road.

Turn right, then at the next road junction right again, but only for a few yards, because on the other side you will see a footpath signpost pointing the way between houses. The path soon bears left, and a few yards further on ignore a path forking right. Soon the path bears right again to cross the old railway line by a stone bridge. Cross the stile at the far side and bear left along a clear path which leads forward and up to a stile, then another stile with a modern house ahead. Bear right up to another stile to the left of a gate and a garage, and walk past the righthand side of the house and up the drive to a stile and another motor road.

Cross straight over to the signposted path to Yorkgate. Cross the stile and bear half-right uphill, keeping to the right of the wood. About 15 yards to the left of the first of the two pylons between you and the house there is a marker post pointing up what is now developing into a clear path, about 10 yards to the left of another clear path leading to the house ahead. The path is almost a hollow way as it bears left and climbs quite steeply to a wall at the top. There are superb views back over Wharfedale as you climb. Cross the stile, then in a couple of yards another stile, and keep forward through the yard to another wooden stile ahead. Cross this and keep on, now with a wall to your left. Cross another stile in the far corner of this field and walk forward across the next field to the stile by a gate and a footpath sign.

Ignore the road going left (Yorkgate) and follow the road straight forward. Ignore the next road on the right and keep on uphill. Shortly after the road bears left at the top of the hill a bridleway sign points right down a walled lane, tarmac as far as the farm. Follow the track down to the next motor road, ignoring a footpath sign pointing left halfway down. Motorists will find their cars on the left.

[*] Cross straight over the road and continue down the track (signposted Intake Farm). Ignore the access road to the farm on the right. Cross the bridge over the Leeds-Ilkley railway and follow the track and then the tarmac road to the A65, where those coming by bus started the walk. Motorists will turn right along the road and at the traffic lights turn left into Bingley road, then jump to the start of the walk description above.

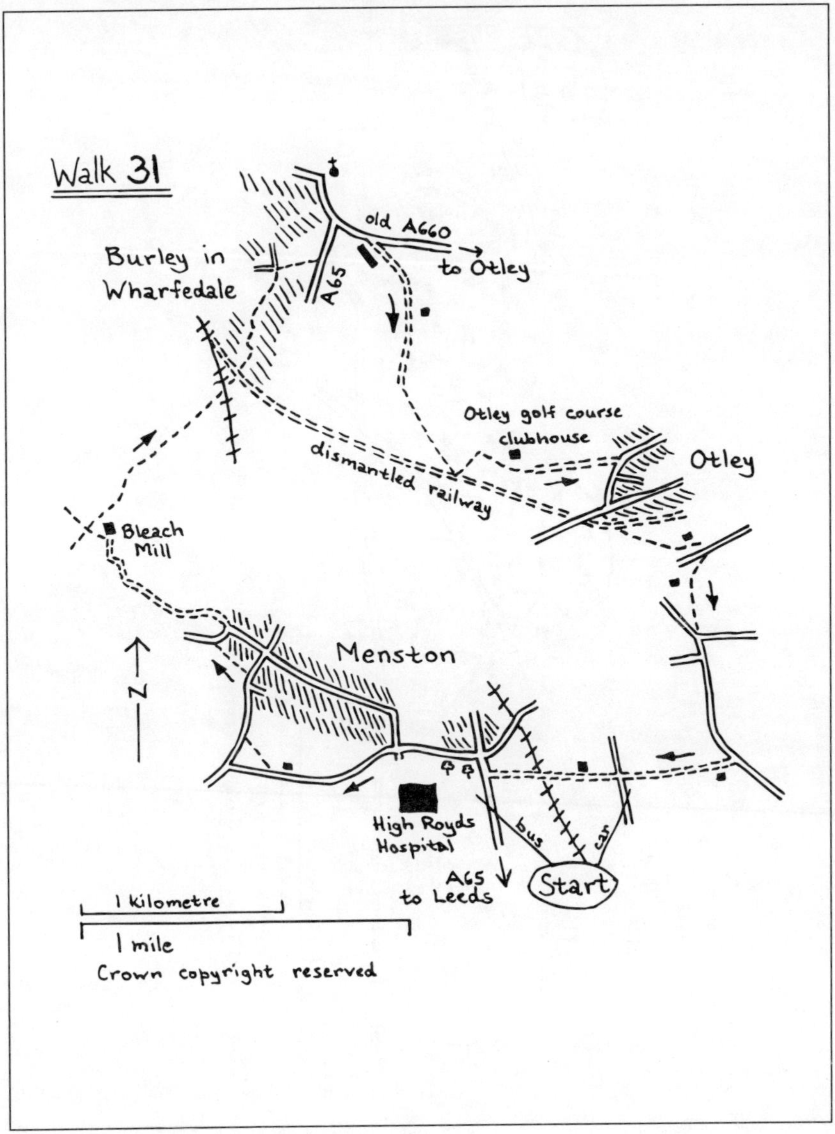

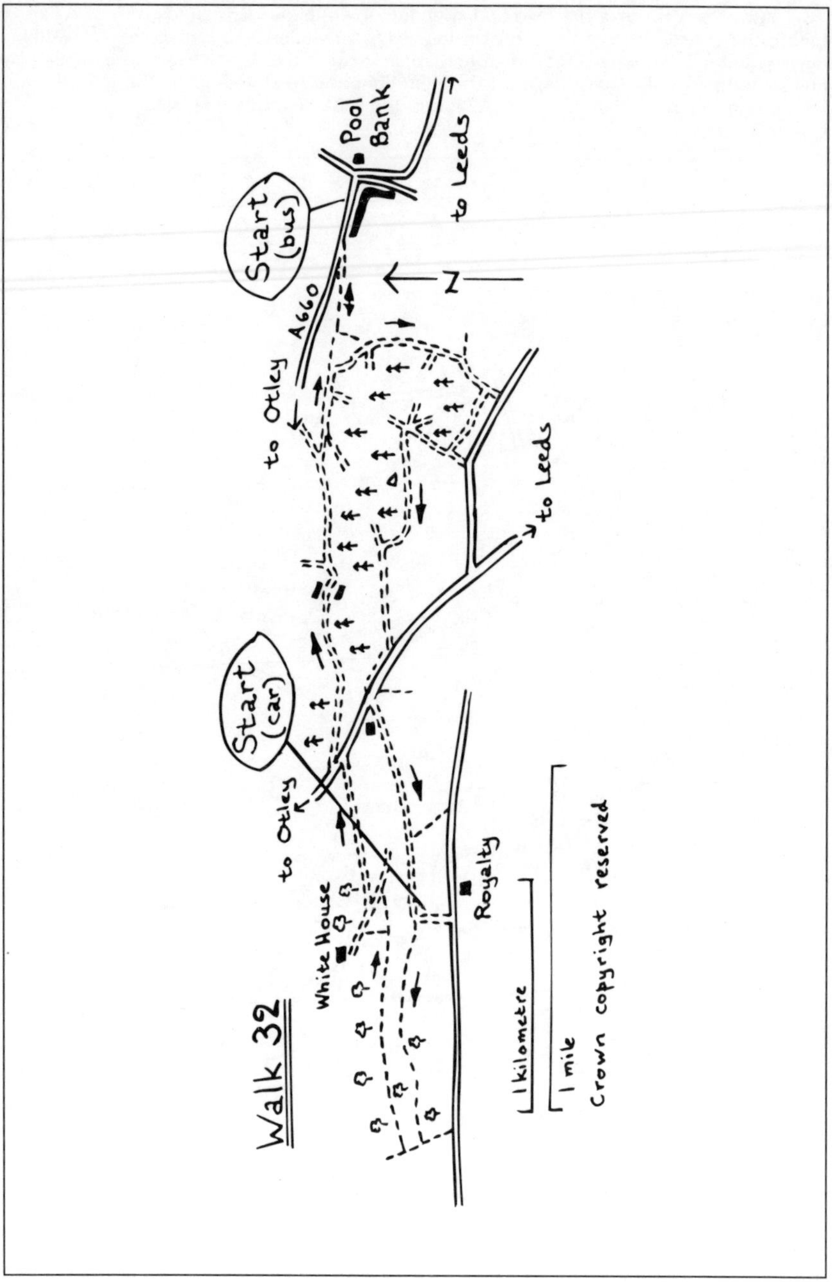

Walk 32
Start (car)
Start (bus)
to Otley
A660
to Otley
Pool Bank
to Leeds
to Leeds
N
White House
Royalty
1 kilometre
1 mile
Crown copyright reserved

THE CHEVIN FOREST PARK

WALK 32

5 miles (8 km); Pathfinder 672 (SE 24/34), 671 (SE 04/14). Otley Chevin is worth exploring in detail – there are lots of paths – and this suggested circuit is intended merely to serve as an introduction. Clear woodland and moorland tracks and paths, with superb views over Lower Wharfedale.

By bus: No. 780 (Otley), X84/784 (Ilkley/Skipton) bus from Leeds Central Bus Station. Alight near the sharp bend with the old Toll Bar House at the top of Pool Bank.
By car: park in the Beacon House car park near the Royalty Inn on Yorkgate (which leaves the Otley old road by the sign for the Chevin Lodge Hotel), walk forward to the Surprise View, turn left and start the walk at [*] below.

From the bus stop walk for 50 yards towards Otley and fork left up Quarry Road, ignoring a footpath ascending steps on the left and a few yards further on keeping right at the fork past a notice saying Private Land No Through Road. Follow the road between houses, and past the garages continue up the track, taking care not to trip over the chain which may be stretched across it. When you are faced by a wooden fence with a large gate in it, take the paved path to the right of the fence. At once there is a splendid view over Wharfedale. When the paving ends keep forward on the narrow footpath, and when you reach the first of two tall wooden pylons fork left on a path heading away from the edge, with a fence on the left at first. When you reach a junction at the wood bear left with the wood to your right.

[#] Ignore a track on the right along a firebreak with a row of power line poles in it, and soon you are walking parallel to another row of power lines on your right. Ignore another track forking right and soon you are at the top of the estate with a high wall to your left. The track bears right away from the wall. When you reach a T-junction by a map-board bear right, and at the fork which follows immediately keep left. At an open space by a wall corner which is a major junction of tracks keep left along the track parallel to the wall on the left with a conifer plantation to your right. You pass a trig point a few yards to the right of the track. After a time the track bears right and descends through the wood. At the next T-junction keep left. The track leads to a car park and the Otley old road.

Turn right down the road. Ignore the first footpath signpost on the left (to Carlton), but follow the second one pointing up a track (to West Chevin Road). (A pleasant alternative to the roadside walk is the path that meanders down through the trees parallel to the road, exiting at a point opposite the West Chevin Road track.) The track leads to a stile by a large gate into the Forest Park (Miller Lane Gate) with a map-board. Keep forward along the track and at the point where a path comes in from the left over a stile ignore a path forking right. Soon there is a fine view down to Otley and up Wharfedale. A field's length away to the left is the Royalty pub, reachable by crossing the next stile on the left and walking through the car park (where motorists will find their cars).

[*] Take the contouring path to the right of the small rocky outcrop ahead, and some distance after passing the rocks keep left at a fork on a path close to a fence on the left. Follow the main contouring path to enter woodland and soon you are walking close to the lefthand edge of the Park with a wall to your left and a view towards Yeadon, Guiseley and Menston. The path drops slightly into the wood but keeps roughly in the same direction, soon with low crags to the left. There are several paths, any of which will do, provided you keep on in the same direction, heading towards the far end of the wood. About 200 yards before you reach the far end the path bears left up to a stile in the wall (through it lies Menston, Ilkley and the Dales and Ebor Ways). Do not cross this, but with your back to the stile follow the path straight down into the wood.

Just before the ground steepens look right and you will see an old wall heading away from you through the wood. Fork right, cross this wall and bear right alongside it, with a steep drop to your left. Now keep close to the edge, climbing gently; the old wall ends. Pass through a gap in a facing wall and now there is an old wall to your left. You cross another old wall coming down the hillside with a path beside it. After a time the wall on your left takes the form of heavy stone slabs set on end. At the end of this section either descend the long flight of steps on the left, at the foot bearing left down the track, or if your knees can't face that keep forward until you reach a track slanting back downhill on the left. The track leads to the White House Information Centre and tearoom.

Return up the track, this time ignoring the steps, but bearing left at the first major fork beyond them along a contouring path. After some time ignore a grassy track forking left and keep forward with crags to your right. The track leads to the East Chevin Quarry car park. Walk through the carpark to the Otley old road and turn left downhill. In 150 yards take the signposted track on the right into the Danefield Estate. Keep on the main track until you pass some workshops and cross a stone bridge with a deep ravine to the left, and then take care not to fork left downhill. The track begins to climb, and soon the view over Wharfedale opens out and you have crags to your right (a favourite practice ground for local climbers). Ignore another track forking left downhill. At the top of the hill you are joined by another track from the right. At the next fork beside the picnic table and an old stone gatepost keep straight forward along the edge of the escarpment. About 100 yards before tall wooden pylons there is a path junction. Go a few yards left to the edge. The magnificent view extends from Otley via Farnley Hall with the Washburn valley beyond and the lakes in the old gravel pits at Knotford Nook to Pool, Almscliff Crag and the Weeton railway viaduct.

Those who came by bus will want to take the path just to the right of the pylons, there re-joining their outward route, motorists will take the path at right-angles to the escarpment, heading towards the wood. After 150 yards the path bears left towards the corner of the wood. When you reach a junction of paths keep forward with the wood to your right. Now follow the description from [#] above.

BRAMHOPE TO COOKRIDGE

WALK 33

5 miles (8 km); Pathfinder 672 (SE24/34); easy tracks and field paths with remarkably distant views.

By bus: *No. 780 (Otley), X84/784 (Ilkley/Skipton) from Leeds Central Bus Station. Alight near Bramhope Church and walk along the road towards the church, but just before you reach it go through the kissing-gate on the left by the notice board and follow the tarmac path past the east end of the church. Where the tarmac ends keep forward over the grass, pass through the trees and keep forward, mount the steps and keep on over more grass to a tarmac drive. Follow this forward, bearing left and right with it, to reach Eastgate, there turning left.*
By car: *From the crossroads by the Fox and Hounds in the centre of Bramhope village take the road signposted to Bradford (Old Lane) and after 100 yards turn right into the free car park (with toilets) (GR 247 433). To start the walk return to Old Lane and turn left along it to the crossroads, there going straight over and along Eastgate.*

In Eastgate look out for the attractive 17th century Weaver's Cottage on the right. Immediately after the parade of shops on the right with the post office take the signposted tarmac path on the right. The mound to the left with the children's playground on top is a spoil heap from the construction of the Bramhope railway tunnel in 1846-9, the line of which we shall be following for the next mile. Cross straight over the first street you reach to continue on a clear path, now on top of the mound of spoil. Soon you descend a flight of steps on the left and bear right to a stile.

The clear path leads forward. Keep left at a fork to another stile; again you are on the raised line of spoil, and you have a fence to your right. Pass to the left of the first of the four tunnel air shafts we shall encounter and keep forward with a wall to your right. Pass between two old gateposts and continue to a stile by some houses. Bear right along the drive to the road, there going left. About 20 yards past Moorland Road on the right cross the signposted stile on the right and bear half-left, passing well to the left of the second air shaft. Pass a redundant stile and keep on the same line to pass between two gorse-covered mounds of spoil. On emerging from these bear slightly left towards the next air shaft, crossing a stile on the way to it. Pass to the right of the air shaft, and the next stile is at the lefthand end of the wood ahead. Keep straight forward, soon again between spoil heaps, to the Otley Old Road.

Cross diagonally right to the stile opposite. Follow the wall, then the fence, on the left, and when faced by a wooden fence ahead turn right along it. In this fence you will come to a short section of wall with a stile in it: cross this and bear half-right up the large field, in the direction of the fourth and last air shaft, to a stile in the top corner. Turn left on the track to cross a stile by a gate, and when the metalled track ends keep forward along the righthand edge of the field. At the far end cross a stile into a fenced path and pass to the left of Crag House Farm. At the end of the fenced path continue by the wall on your right to a stile by a gate. Turn left along the farm access road.

When you reach the grounds of Cookridge Cricket Club turn right along the tarmac lane, keeping the cricket ground on your left. When the tarmac bears right into Kings Lea, keep straight ahead along the dirt track. The track curves right, then left again. Pass to the right of Moseley Farm and downhill, to cross Moseley Beck and the Leeds to Harrogate railway line (glance right to see the entrance to the Bramhope Tunnel). Follow the path uphill, passing to the left of a derelict redbrick mill and to the right of some cottages. At the top of the hill the track bears right through the yard of Dean Grange Farm and shortly afterwards bears left again, passing a subterranean building on the right. A few yards past this fork right off the track up the bank to a stile by a gate.

Walk along near the edge of the field with a wall to your left, cross the stile in the field corner and bear right along the edge of the next field, now with the wall to your right.

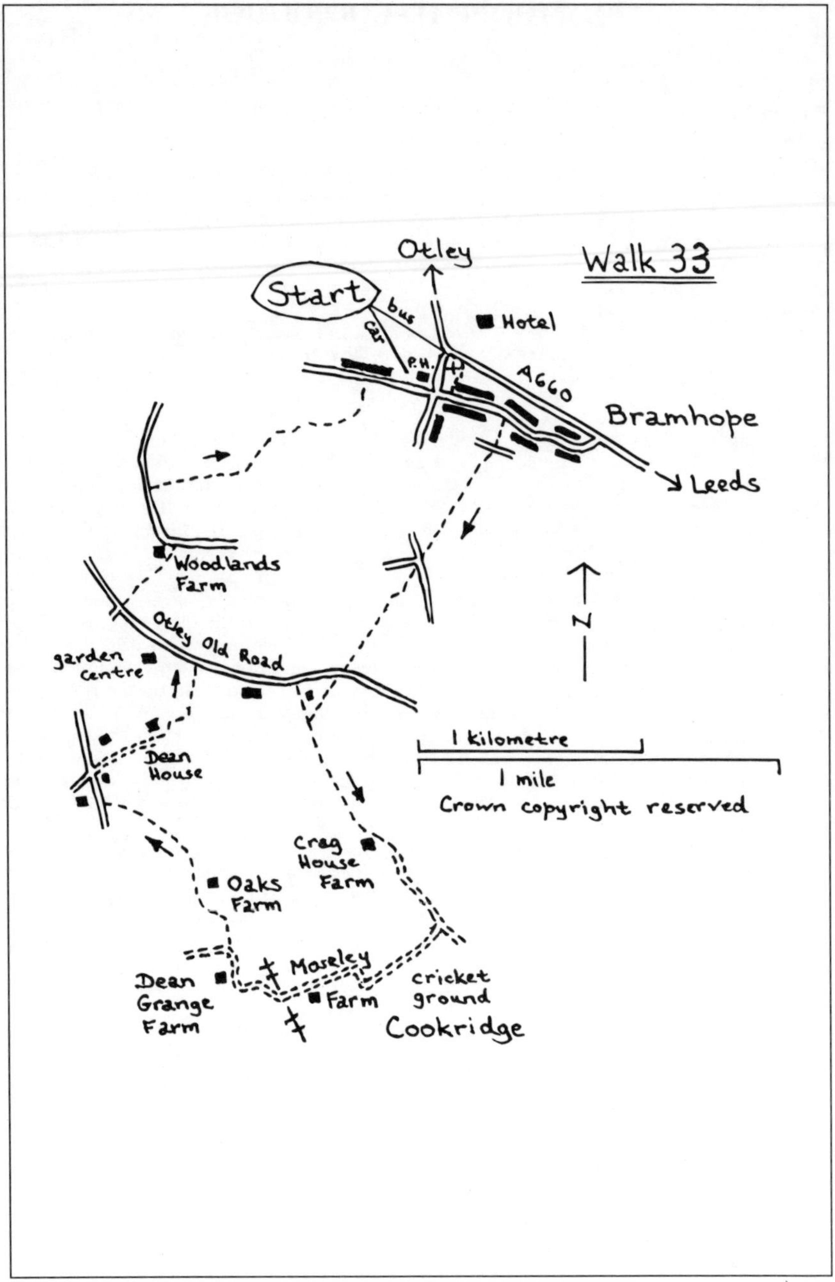
Walk 33
Otley
Start
bus
car
P.H.
Hotel
A660
Bramhope
Leeds
Woodlands Farm
Otley Old Road
garden centre
N
1 kilometre
1 mile
Crown copyright reserved
Dean House
Crag House Farm
Oaks Farm
Moseley Farm
Dean Grange Farm
cricket ground
Cookridge

Bear left at the end of the field towards the wood, and when you reach it enter it over the broken down wall on the right. The clear path bears slightly left and then right to emerge from the wood by a step-stile. Cross the plank bridge and bear left to the tarmac access road to Oaks Farm; turn right along it, but where it bears right to drop to the farm keep straight forward on a clear track. At the end of the field ignore a track forking left uphill and keep forward through the gate, then bearing left along the edge of the next field on a faint track. Cross the stile by the gate in the field corner and bear left round the edge of the next field, ignoring the gate in the next corner and turning right with the edge of the field and the wall to your left. Cross the stile in the next corner and keep forward along a narrow fenced path (this may be so overgrown that most walkers keep to the left of it) to reach Scotland Lane over a stile.

Turn right along the road. In 200 yards at the next road junction turn right down the stony access road to Dean Head. Keep straight down, ignoring tracks forking left and right to houses, and at the bottom keep forward, passing to the right of Dean House, through a gate into a fenced path. Cross a beck and keep forward into a wood. The clear path keeps close to the lefthand edge of the wood and leaves it by a stile. Bear left up the edge of the field to re-emerge onto the Otley Old Road over a stile. Turn left, pass High Trees Garden Centre and a layby much used by plane spotters, and in a few yards at the road junction cross the signposted stile on the right and walk down the field with the wall to your left.

Cross the stile and footbridge in the bottom and head straight on, up towards Woodlands Farm. Cross a stile by a gate in the wall on the right just below the farm and follow the garden wall on your left to the corner, there going left with it to cross another stile and pass to the right of the farmhouse to another stile and the road. Bear left up the road. In about 300 yards ignore a signposted path on the left, but 60 yards further on cross the stile on the right (also signposted) and follow the edge of the field with a wall to your right. At the end of the field turn left with the wall and 15 yards from the corner cross the step-stile in it. Walk straight across the next field towards some trees (fine views ahead and to the right). Cross the next stile and bear slightly left away from the field edge on a faint path, with Bramhope visible ahead. Cross the stile and cut the corner of the next field to a plank bridge, stile and footpath sign. Keep on the same line, diagonally across the next large field, to a stile in the far corner. Now follow the wall on your left (abundant nettles in summer!) soon entering an old hedged/walled way, which leads back to Old Lane in Bramhope. Turn right to return to the starting point.

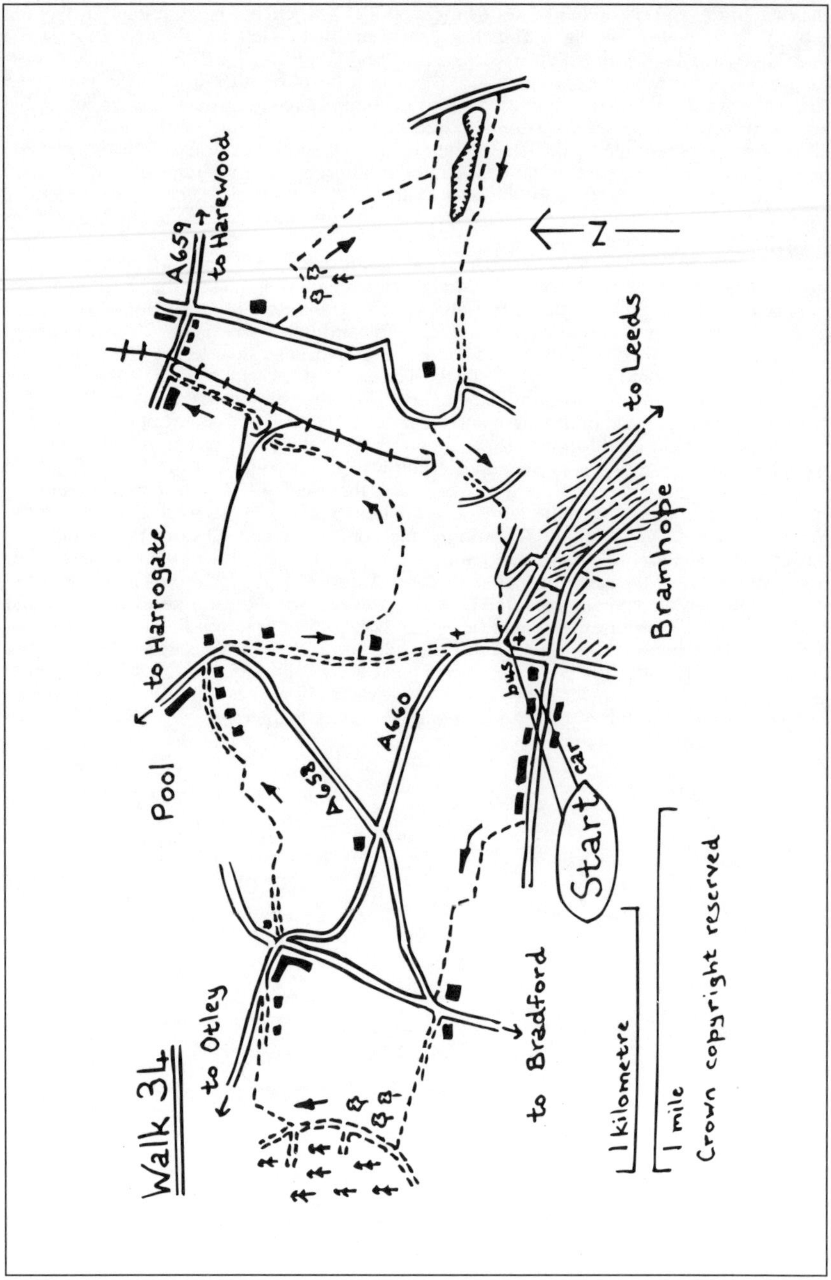
Walk 34
to Otley
to Bradford
Pool
A658
A660
to Harrogate
A659
to Harewood
N
bus
car
Start
Bramhope
to Leeds
1 kilometre
1 mile
Crown copyright reserved

BRAMHOPE, POOL BANK AND ARTHINGTON BANK

WALK 34

3½ or 6 miles (5½ or 9½ km); Pathfinder 672 (SE24/34); a mixture of tracks and field and woodland paths with good views; several quite steep descents, and several busy main roads to cross.

By bus: *No. 780 (Otley), X84/784 (Ilkley/Skipton) from Leeds Central Bus Station. Alight at Bramhope Church, and keeping the church on your left walk up Church Hill to the crossroads at the top, there turning right past the Fox and Hounds along Old Lane.*
By car: *From the crossroads by the Fox and Hounds in the centre of Bramhope village take the road signposted to Bradford (Old Lane) and after 100 yards turn right into the free car park (with toilets) (GR 247 433). To start the walk return to Old Lane and turn right along it.*

Continue along Old Lane as far as the last house on the right. Immediately beyond this turn right along the signposted footpath. At the end of the walled section bear left and cross a stile, continuing with a broken wall to your left and passing through an old gateway en route. After going through another gateway cross the next field diagonally right to a stile by a massive old stone gatepost, after which you follow the wall on your right to the tennis courts of Hilton Grange School. To the right of these a ginnel leads to the busy A658 Bradford to Harrogate road. Cross this with great care and go left for 15 yards before turning right along a track (note the Ebor Way signpost: the Ebor Way links the Cleveland Way at Helmsley with the Dales Way at Ilkley).

Cross a stile by a gate and follow the track to its end, here crossing the stile between two gates and following the wall on the left to another stile into the wood. Follow the clear path along the lefthand edge of the wood, and when you reach a cross track by a line of overhead cables turn right along it. You are now in the Danefield Estate, part of the Chevin Forest Park, owned by Leeds Metropolitan Council. In a few yards ignore a track forking left, and shortly after you pass under the power lines ignore another track forking left. When the track forks into three by a gate and stile, cross the stile and keep forward on the middle branch, and at the next fork keep right, down to the edge of Caley Crags, from where there is a superb view over Lower Wharfedale.

Now return to the cross track a few yards from the edge and turn left along it (if you hadn't gone forward to the edge you would of course have turned right along this track) towards two massive pylons, by the second of which there is a path junction: keep left, i.e. straight ahead, on a narrow path which drops a little and runs along some way below the edge of the escarpment. When you reach a track, with a large gate on the right, turn left down it and follow it to the A660 Leeds to Otley road. Cross this with care and turn right to the next corner. (Buses back to Bramhope/Leeds are available from here.) Ignore Old Pool Bank on the left, but immediately after the Bar House (site of a former toll bar) turn left along the track (signposted). Having entered woodland the track begins to descend, passes a sort of layby on the left by a rocky outcrop and curves slightly left: just before this curve look out for a narrow but clear path forking right. This soon reaches a broader path at a T-junction: bear left here and soon emerge by some houses. Pass the righthand end of these and keep forward back into the wood on a clear narrow path.

This area was extensively quarried in the past, which explains the up and down nature of the terrain. There are several steep descents on the path, but its route is never in doubt. Shortly after one of these descents look for a stile in a fence ahead of you on the edge of the wood: cross this and follow the path forward across a field. On your right you will see an avenue of chestnut trees and the path leads into this; cross a stile and follow the avenue down to the A658 Bradford to Harrogate road once more. Having passed under the arch, look up to discover the name of the chestnut avenue: Avenue des Hirondelles. Cross the road: take care, because your view right is restricted and the traffic comes down fast, and turn right up the footway. Pass the entrance to Firs Hill Court and keep left past the post box into a descending tarmac lane, which leads to the right of a large house, then narrows and starts to climb steeply.

This is Staircase Lane, and for the shorter walk you must follow it all the way to the main road, where you can catch a bus back to Leeds, or to return to the car bear left past the 17th century Puritan chapel and fork right at Bramhope parish church up Church Hill to Bramhope Cross.

For the longer walk, climb Staircase Lane until just before the tarmac starts at Staircase House: here a footpath signpost points left along a track to a stile by a gate. A faint track continues half-right across the field to a gate in the far corner; ignore a kissing-gate on the right and walk down the righthand edge of the next field to another kissing-gate in the far corner, which gives access to a fenced path. Follow this to its end and another kissing-gate; now bear slightly left down a shallow valley, soon joining a clear track which you follow down to the field corner. Now walk along with a fence to the left and a row of sycamores to the right to a stile a few yards to the left of a gate, which gives access to a grassy track.

The railway to your right is the Leeds to Harrogate line, which has just emerged from the Bramhope Tunnel. Follow the track until you reach a fork, where a track on the right leads over a stile by a gate and through a tunnel (above was the old line to Otley). Soon you reach another gate with a stile beside it: bear left down the wide unsurfaced road to the A659 Pool to Harewood road and turn right along it under the railway bridge (there is a footway on the other side). Take the next minor road on the right (Creskeld Lane) and follow it until you reach a public footpath sign on the left (to Black Hill Road). Cross the stile and walk diagonally right across the field (this can be wet!) towards the far corner, where a post and wire fence on the left meets the wooden fence with the wood behind it on the right: in this corner is a stile; cross this and walk along with the wood to your right until you reach a gate which leads to a fenced footpath through a narrow piece of woodland to another gate.

Now bear half-right, towards the corner of wood projecting into the field; having passed it, you will see a kissing-gate in the fence ahead. Pass through and bear very slightly left up the slope; there is no path. There is an extensive view back over Lower Wharfedale. As you get higher, you will see that you are heading for a hedge, which ends in a few yards of fencing in the middle of the field. Pass this corner and continue uphill with the fence to your right. The fence becomes a wall, which you follow up to a stone step-stile by a gate. Keep uphill along the righthand edge of the field; ignore a gate on the right, and now you have a wood to your right. Follow the wall up to the corner, where there is a stile into the wood. Turn left on the path along the edge of the wood. At the motor road turn right up to the top of Arthington Bank, ignoring the entrance to Arthington Quarry on the right.

About 150 yards after the road levels out take the signposted bridleway on the right, a rather narrow and sometimes muddy path. Soon you can see the scale of the quarry workings on your right and for a time the path broadens into a track. Pass through a gate and keep forward, following a ditch on the left. Bramhope is visible ahead, with the Forte Crest Hotel prominent. The path becomes a track, which leads to a motor road, Creskeld Lane again. Turn right along it as far as a signposted bridleway on the left, opposite a gate in the wall on the right.

The path leads eventually to a tarmac drive: follow this up to the street and cross straight over to the continuation of the bridleway. This also leads to a tarmac drive and another street: here keep your line, diagonally right across it, to the tarmac continuation of the bridleway. The tarmac soon ends, but follow the path up to the next street and turn right along it. On the next rising lefthand bend the bridleway forks right, with a ravine to the right, and leads back up to the A660 on the bend opposite Bramhope Parish Church. From here either catch a bus back to Leeds or cross the road with great care and walk up Church Hill to the cross, there turning right to return to your car. N.B. At the time of writing the last section of this bridleway from the rising lefthand bend is temporarily closed for essential repairs, so you must continue up the road (Hall Rise) to the main road. There is a bus stop a few yards to the right, or to return to your car cross the main road and turn right for 30 yards to a signposted ginnel on the left which leads to the main street in Bramhope village. Turn right and follow this back to the Cross.

GOLDEN ACRE TO HAREWOOD

WALK 35

9 miles (14.5 km); Pathfinder 672 (SE24/34); Golden Acre, one of Leeds City Council's showpiece parks, is popular with gardeners, children who like feeding ducks, birdwatchers who like looking at them, dog-walkers, indeed anyone who enjoys walking in beautiful and well-cared for surroundings. Our walk uses field paths, tracks and short stretches of minor road to link Golden Acre to Harewood Park, another piece of fine landscape on a somewhat larger scale.

By bus: No. 780/784 Otley/Ilkley bus from Leeds Central Bus Station to Golden Acre Park. Having got off the bus, don't cross the main road to the Park but walk back 100 yards and bear right into the car-park.
By car: Park in the main car-park for Golden Acre on the A660 Leeds to Otley road.

Walk to the Leeds end of the car-park, go down the steps and bear left to pass under the main road and enter the Park. Turn left at the T-junction and stay on the main track until you reach a broad tarmac cross-track. Turn right to the Information Centre, café and toilets. Having passed the café keep right at the fork and pass to the right of a bungalow. Immediately before you reach a wooden shelter on the left, fork left off the track and pass to the left of some tall rhododendrons to find a clear path winding upwards to a quiet glade with some benches. The first bench on the right is the Jack Madden Memorial seat.

Now return to the main track and continue past the shelter. At the next fork keep left and head for a wooden gate leading out of Golden Acre. Turn left up the track. You reach the road at a junction: cross straight over the first road and take the second one, half-right (King Lane). Where the wood on the left begins, cross the signposted stile and follow the path into the wood. The path keeps close to the fence on the left. Cross another stile and keep forward through the wood. Never far from the lefthand edge of the wood, the path leads to another road. Turn left along it. A few yards before the next house on the right, turn right along the signposted track. By a footpath sign the track turns sharp right towards Lineham Farm. Pass through the wide gateway into the old farmyard and in a few yards a sign points half-right: follow the fenced path along to a stile, then keep by the fence on the left to another stile. Walk straight across the middle of the next field to a stile just to the right of a gate on the far side. Keep forward over the next field, towards the righthand end of the farm ahead, to reach a marker post near a large solitary tree by a gate in the wall on the right. Bear left along the remains of a track, keeping the wall to your right, to another gate ahead. Keep forward on the track for a few more yards, but where it bears right to the farm, fork left off it and make for a stile 5 yards to the right of the gate in the top corner of the field. Cross and follow the hedge/fence on the left to the next footpath sign and road.

The New Inn is a short way left along the road, but we only go left for 20 yards to the next signposted footpath on the right. Cross the stile and bear slightly left, to walk across the middle of this large field. Pass close to a power line pole and keep the same line to a stile in the hedge on the far side. Now follow the hedge on the right to the next stile, and turn left along the track. You are now on the Leeds Country Way. Follow the track to a gate, then on along the righthand edge of the field, but at the next old field boundary follow the signpost sharp left along it. Soon the clear track resumes. After passing through a gate it bears right along the righthand edge of the field. In the next field corner ignore the gate ahead and turn left, still keeping to the righthand edge of the field. Leave this field by a gateway and keep on the clear track as it bears slightly left across the next field. Having passed through another old gateway the track turns sharp right, then soon sharp left again and climbs past Stub House Farm.

When you reach a T-junction the Leeds Country Way goes right, but we take the first track on the left and join the Ebor Way. Look right through the trees for a glimpse of Harewood House. Follow the track to the next road and turn left uphill, with a lovely view right over Lower Wharfedale. Take the first minor road on the right downhill. Ignore a farm

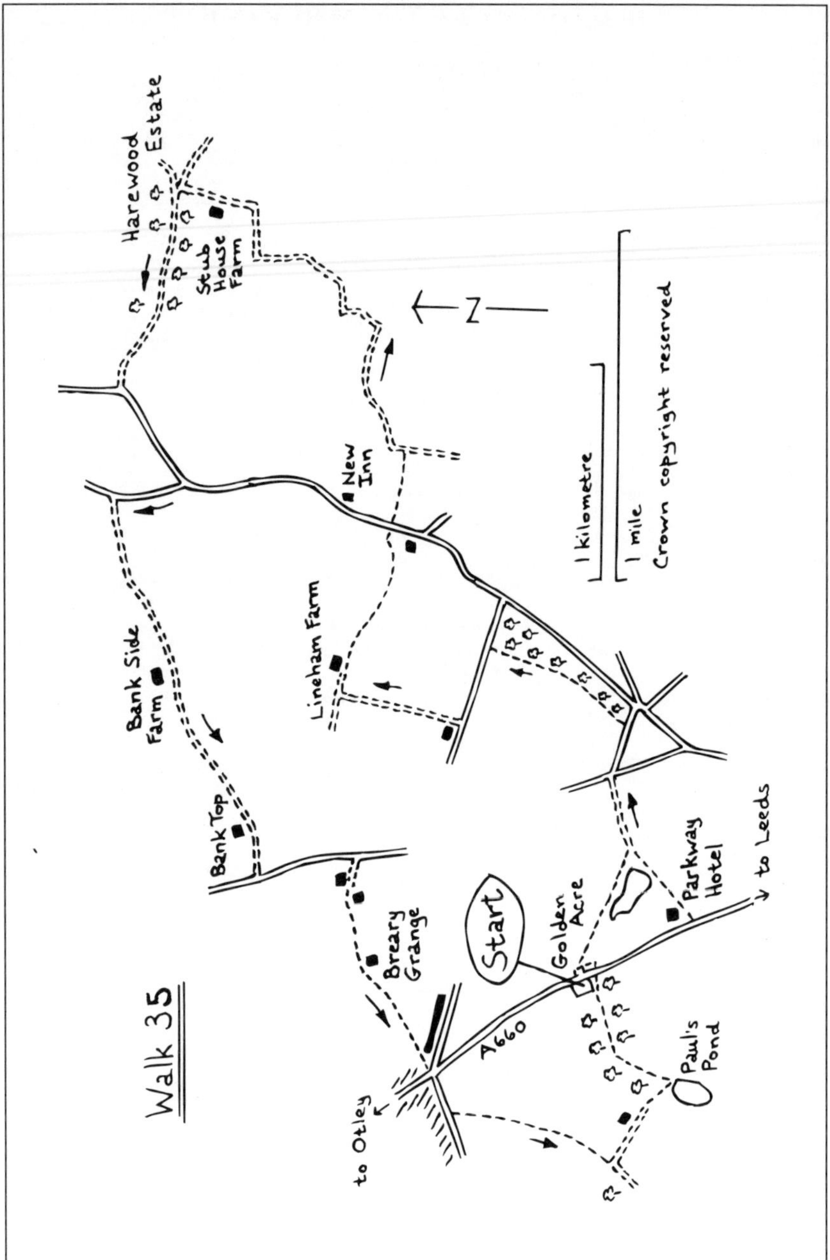
Walk 35
to Otley
A660
Start
Golden Acre
Paul's Pond
Parkway Hotel
to Leeds
Breary Grange
Bank Top
Bank Side Farm
Lineham Farm
New Inn
Harewood Estate
Stub House Farm
N
1 kilometre
1 mile
Crown copyright reserved

entrance on the left but take the next lane on the left, a No Through Road. When the track forks at Bank Side Farm keep straight forward, passing to the right of a barn, on a clear track. Cross a stile by a gate and now you are in an old lane. Cross another stile by a gate and continue up Bank Top Lane. Pass through a large metal gate and follow the track to the left of Bank Top Farm and on to the next road. Turn left.

Take the signposted entrance drive to Breary Cottage on the right. Cross the stile by the gate in front and pass to the right of the next house ahead but to the left of a stone barn. Go through the gate and continue along the lefthand edge of the next field. At the far end there is a stile 20 yards to the right of the gate. Bear slightly right across the middle of the next field to another stile in the fence opposite. Cross both stile and footbridge and walk straight down the lefthand edge of the field to a ladder-stile to the left of a solitary tree. Keep straight forward across the next large field, passing to the left of another solitary tree and making for a stile at the righthand end of a short row of trees in the fence ahead. The stile turns out to be in a fence corner: cross it and keep down parallel to the fence on the left until you have passed the lefthand end of a deep ditch which crosses the field. Now bear slightly right, heading for the righthand corner of the gardens of the houses on the left, where you bear slightly more right towards the Shell Garage on the far side of the main road. Cross the stile and the A660 and take the No Through Road opposite (The Sycamores).

Opposite house number 8 cross the stile on the left and follow the lefthand edge of the field. At the end of the third field cross a stile and now follow the edge of the wood on your right. Pass through a gateway with a redundant stile and turn left along the track. Pass to the right of the derelict farm and follow the fence forward to a stile into the wood. Bear half-right, ignoring the path more sharply right parallel to the edge of the wood. Soon a path climbs an embankment on the right to Paul's Pond. Turn left along the edge of the pond, but only as far as the next corner, where you fork left again and drop to cross a plank bridge over a beck. Bear left on the waymarked path (Leeds Country Way) parallel to the edge of the wood. Pass through a wooden barrier and bear right along a broad track. Having passed a board with a map of the Breary Marsh Nature Reserve you enter a fenced boardwalk which leads back to your starting point.

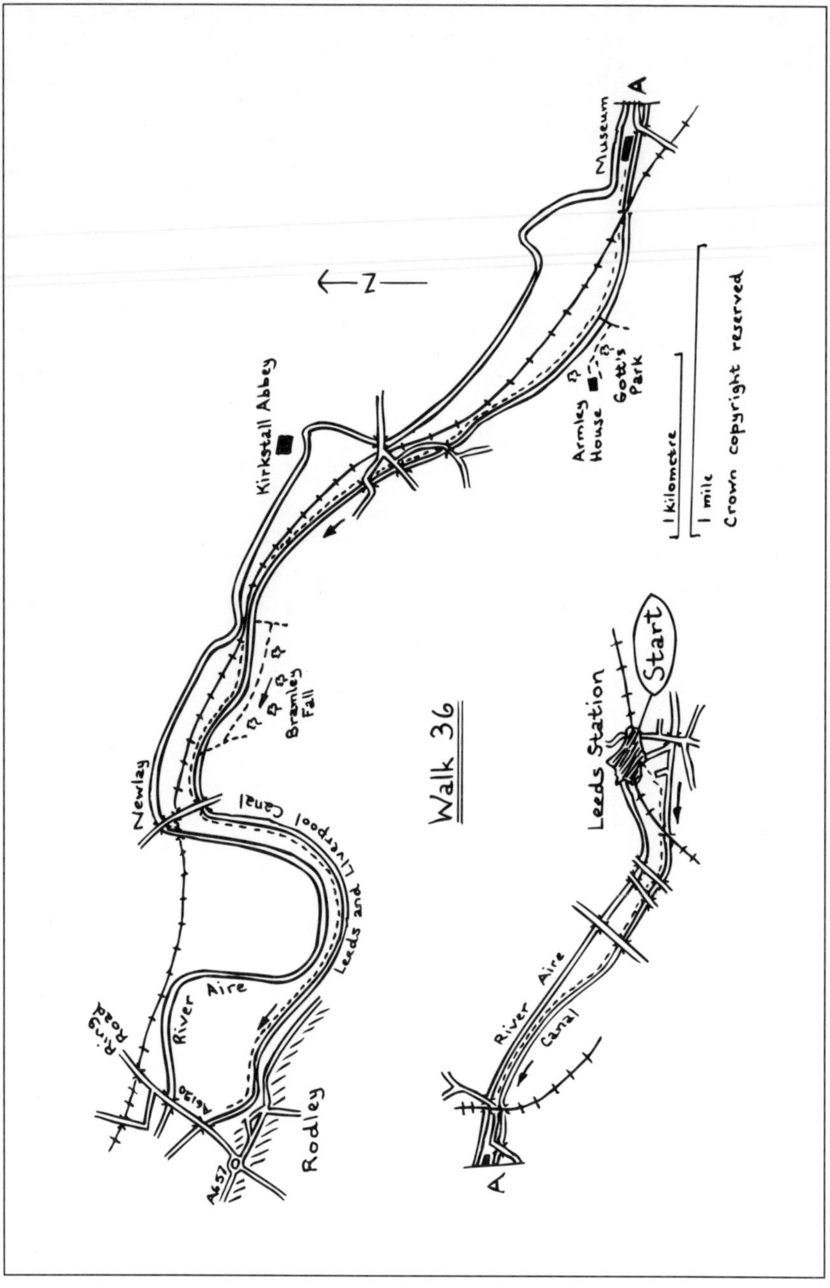
Walk 36
Start
Leeds Station
River Aire
Canal
A
Museum
N
Kirkstall Abbey
Armley House
Gott's Park
1 kilometre
1 mile
Crown copyright reserved
Bramley Fall
Newlay
Leeds and Liverpool Canal
River Aire
Ring Road
A6120
A657
Rodley
A

THE LEEDS AND LIVERPOOL CANAL

WALK 36

The basic towpath walk is 6½ miles (10½ km), but there is so much to see on the way and there are so many interesting detours that I suggest you make a day of it! Pathfinder 683 (SE23/33). I have used parts of the route in Walks 27 and 37, but as this ramble from the city centre to Rodley is a Leeds classic with so much to offer both the historian and the lover of nature I felt I had to include it as a walk in its own right. In 1981 the Leeds City Council established the Museum of Leeds Trail along this route, and I am indebted to its guidebook for much of the historical information in what follows.

Buy a Day Rover and leave your car at home for this one! The walk starts at Leeds Station and finishes at Rodley, from where buses 760, 670, 671 will return you to Leeds Central Bus Station and 81, 82 will take you to Horsforth and Holt Park.

On emerging from Leeds Station walk straight over the pedestrian crossing to a small white tower building with a sign saying Way Out Bishopgate, go down the steps and turn right to follow the road under the station. Turn right through the arches leading to Granary Wharf, and cross the Aire, which flows under the station, just before entering the Wharf shopping precinct. After exploring the interesting collection of shops make your way to the car park alongside and turn right along the pavement. At the end of the car park you reach the Leeds Canal Basin. Bear left to the 18th century bridge over the canal with the canal company's original office behind it, but without crossing the bridge keep forward along the towpath. The two 19th century Italianate campaniles on the other side belong to the Tower Works.

Bridge 225G is Monk Bridge of 1886, with the city arms incorporated into its ironwork. The next impressive stone bridge with the very large arch and balustrade was built in 1846 for the Leeds and Thirsk Railway. Pass under the bridge, and just after the St.Ann's Ing Lock, on the other side of the canal, are the long low brick railway workshops with the large round-headed windows. The next concrete bridge carries the Inner Ring Road, and when you emerge from it your eye is caught by the large brick Castleton Mill of 1838 with its semi-circular stair tower. Having passed Spring Garden Locks, the massive wall on the other side of the canal is part of the foundations of the 19th century Leeds Forge. The next very striking feature is the Leeds and Thirsk Railway viaduct built in 1846. Continuing, look out for the attractive cast-iron balustrade of the Canal Road Bridge, now on a modern concrete base. To visit Armley Mills, the Leeds Industrial Museum, which is straight ahead of you after you pass under the Canal Road Bridge, turn right immediately after the bridge through the arch and up the steps, then turn right again to cross the bridge and right again into the museum car park.

Our walk continues along the towpath. The arched stone bridge 225, giving access to the museum, dates from the 1770s. At the end of the high wall enclosing the museum turn right to the viewpoint over the River Aire: the large mill dam is conspicuous, and looking right there is a good view of the museum itself. Pass under the railway bridge, and soon two concrete bridges carry the towpath over the entrances to Power Station Wharf, where barges used to bring the coal for Kirkstall Power Station, but which is now a quiet backwater. The towpath is now quite rural, with the wooded Gott's Park across the canal. For a detour through the Park, landscaped by Humphrey Repton, to the classical Armley House, once the residence of Benjamin Gott, the owner of Armley Mills, cross the next stone bridge (224) and immediately turn right off the drive, in about 15 yards forking left on a clear climbing path which soon bears right and rises through the woods to a flight of steps. At the top you emerge into the open Park, now occupied by a golf course, and by following the path round the edge of the wood on your right you reach two tarmac paths, either of which will take you to the house, which now serves as the clubhouse for the golf course and also contains a café. Notice the fine views back to the city centre and up the valley to Kirkstall Abbey and beyond. Return by the same route to the canal towpath.

When you reach a bridge preceded by a grassy space with benches and a car park, a detour to Kirkstall Abbey is possible: the route is described in Walk 37. Our walk continues along the towpath. The large building on the other side of the canal by the bridge is the former Kirkstall Brewery, from which last century beers were carried down the canal to Goole and exported to Australia and New Zealand. Bridge 221A is the Leeds and Bradford Road Bridge, and after it look right for views of Kirkstall Abbey, the best probably being the one from Kirkstall Lock. From the three-rise Forge Locks the buildings of Kirkstall Forge, once an important iron foundry, can be seen across the railway and the river. Here too another detour is possible through Bramley Fall, 100 acres of woodland owned by the City Council, an area once extensively quarried: it was from here that the stone came to build Kirkstall Abbey. The woodland paths while attractive are often muddy, and the drier alternative is to remain on the towpath.

If you do decide to make the detour, cross the canal by the top lock and the overflow channel by the footbridge, and ignoring the flight of steps ahead bear right along a clear path. At a fork keep left on the main path which climbs gently through the woods, and at the next fork again keep left to climb some steps to a signpost and a broad cross track. Turn right along this, and walking parallel to the canal below you on the right, follow it all the way to another footpath sign (look out for drier paths to the side of the track which have formed to avoid some of the muddy sections) where another broad track comes in from the left and Newlay Locks are to your right. Keep forward to the locks and re-cross the canal by the lock gate. Resume your journey along the towpath.

At the next stone road bridge (221) a detour is possible right to the 18th century Abbey Inn and the charming Newlay Bridge (see Walk 37), but our route continues along the towpath (we have now been joined by Walk 27). Shortly after passing the marina the Georgian Whitecote House is seen across the canal. Follow the towpath all the way to Rodley, and having passed the Rodley Barge on the other side of the canal, cross the canal by the swing bridge and turn left along Dalmeny Terrace to pass the inn and reach the main road. Turn right for a short distance for the bus stop for buses back to Leeds (there are toilets opposite), and a little further on the other side of the road is the stop for buses to Horsforth, Cookridge and Holt Park.

KIRKSTALL ABBEY TO NEWLAY

WALK 37

5½ miles (9 km); Pathfinder 683 (SE23/33). The walk follows almost exactly one of the suggested walks through the Kirkstall Valley Park, and is waymarked almost throughout by a blue square inside a yellow arrow. The Abbey itself, the Abbey House Museum and the Lapidarium in the abbey grounds are all worth a visit.

By bus: No. 732, 733, 734, 735, 736 Otley/Ilkley bus from Leeds Central Bus Station to Kirkstall Abbey. Cross the main road to the car park opposite the Abbey House Museum off Abbey Walk.
By car: Park in the Kirkstall Abbey car park opposite the Abbey House Museum off Abbey Walk (GR 259 363).

Having explored the Abbey, Museum and Lapidarium, walk towards the far side of the car park away from the museum and turn right uphill on the grass with a wood to your right. Keep straight up, to pass through a gap in the hedge ahead, cross straight over the road and up Kepstorn Rise. Keep straight over the next street, Kepstorn Close, and up the path into the wood. Bear right, pass between bollards, then bear left over the Leeds to Harrogate railway. Now keep straight forward, ignoring paths to left and right, until near the top side of the wood the path bears right, with houses over to the left. When you reach an old tarmac road leading towards the wood, cross it diagonally right and continue along the tarmac path with houses to the left and the wood to the right. When the wood ends you reach a T-junction: fork left and walk between the houses to reach Queenswood Drive through bollards.

Cross over and continue along Queenswood Road, but after 100 yards, before the next street on the left, go up a tarmac ginnel on the left which soon becomes a path through woodland and bears right with a fence to the right and the wood to the left. When the houses on the right end and you emerge into Beckett Park, keep forward along the righthand edge of the wood. There are swings and a chute down to your right should you need them. The path bears left towards the college; with the college ahead, turn left along a tarmac road, but the tarmac soon ends. With a redbrick building 60 yards ahead, you fork right on a broad track following the sign to the athletics track. Before you reach an open space and another redbrick building, fork left between rhododendrons on a broad track, which soon leads you to an arch commemorating Queen Victoria's visit to Leeds in 1858 for the opening of the Town Hall. Pass to the right of the arch and continue forward, now on a narrow path.

Soon you are joined by another path from the left. At a fork the yellow arrow says you can go either way: I suggest you keep right, to follow the lefthand edge of the playing fields with an iron fence to your left; when you reach a gateway in this with a track descending from it, walk down this towards some more playing fields. Cross a cross path and reach an old stone gatepost. Keep forward across the grass, to pass to the right of some trees; keep these to your left, and where they end bear right along a fence with redbrick houses beyond it. Where the fence turns left, bear slightly left to pass another old stone gatepost in the middle of the grass and reach Spen Lane through a row of trees.

Cross Spen Lane, turn right for a few yards and take the first road on the left (Butcher Hill). When you reach some playing fields on the left, a line of lampposts across the grass indicates the route of the footpath. Near the far end you pass Abbey Grange School and drop to rejoin the road. When the pavement gives out cross the road, ignore the footpath sign pointing right along the bottom of the school grounds and keep forward over the railway bridge. Re-cross the road and continue downhill. Ignore the first road on the left (although the yellow arrow points along it!), but 50 yards further on take a ginnel on the left, which leads to Cragside Close, where you bear right. The street soon bears left, and there is a stile in the fence on the right into Hawksworth Woods (and now you are back with the yellow arrow!).

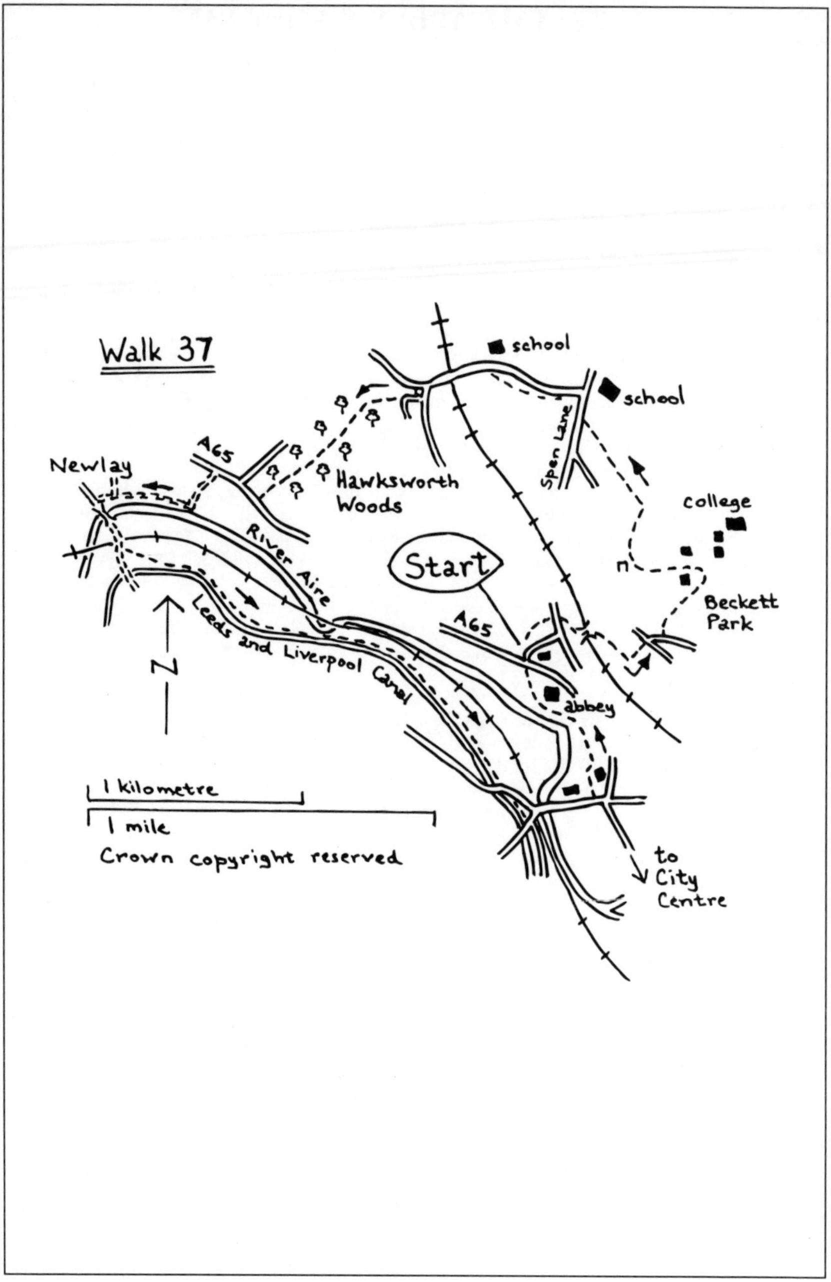
Walk 37
school
school
Spen Lane
A65
Newlay
Hawksworth
Woods
College
River Aire
Start
Beckett
Park
A65
Leeds and Liverpool Canal
N
abbey
1 kilometre
1 mile
Crown copyright reserved
to
City
Centre

Having entered the wood, watch closely for the arrows. Go right at the first fork, left at the second and left at the third, cross straight over a clear cross path and at the next T-junction follow the arrow left. The beck is a short distance to your right. The path leads past some splendidly climbable rocks before being joined by a clear path from the left; ignore a path forking left just after this and drop to the A65. A quick, but boring way back to your starting point would be to turn left along this main road. But we cross it (there is a helpful island a short way to the right) and turn right. A sign soon indicates that we are entering Horsforth. Immediately after the first house on the left turn left down a stony track (bridleway sign). Cross an old mill race just before the track bears right, and now you are close to the river Aire. When you reach a stile by a gate you can hear and glimpse the weir on the left at which the mill race starts. Walk forward and then turn left over the cobbled Newlay Bridge, erected in 1819 and one of the oldest iron bridges in the county. This is a delightful spot.

Now you enter the Kirkstall Valley Park. Keep forward along the road and cross the modern railway bridge (Leeds to Ilkley/Skipton lines); down on the right is the 18th century Abbey Inn. Just beyond the bridge you will see two tracks on the left: take the second of these, but in 5 yards fork right off it beside the map-board on a path which leads up to the towpath of the Leeds and Liverpool Canal. Turn left along this. At Newlay Lock you can either continue along the towpath or cross the canal and the following footbridge to walk through Bramley Fall park. If you choose the latter, bear left on the path and follow it to a fork, where you want to keep left on the 'canal side walk'; in fact you walk parallel to the canal, but some distance from it, at one point rising quite high above it, on a broad woodland path. Ignore two signposted right forks and keep going until you reach a signposted left fork down some steps to Forge Locks. At the foot bear right and re-cross the canal at the locks.

Turn right along the towpath. Soon Kirkstall Abbey is visible over to the left. At the next lock you can move onto a track to the left of the towpath, but make sure you return to it before you pass under the next bridge. The large building across the canal as you continue to the next bridge is the old Kirkstall Brewery. Pass under this bridge too, then bear left before the benches to the road. Go a yard or two left to the T-junction then right along Broad Lane to the traffic lights, passing the Hollybush Farm Conservation Centre, which can be visited. At the traffic lights bear right over the Aire and walk past the Clover store. It is difficult to cross this busy road, so follow it to the traffic lights at the A65, cross it there, then walk back along the other side until you reach a gateway between black railings leading to a track with an old mill goit to one's right. At a fork bear right over the wooden footbridge, then bear left at the next fork to keep off the main road and return to the abbey.

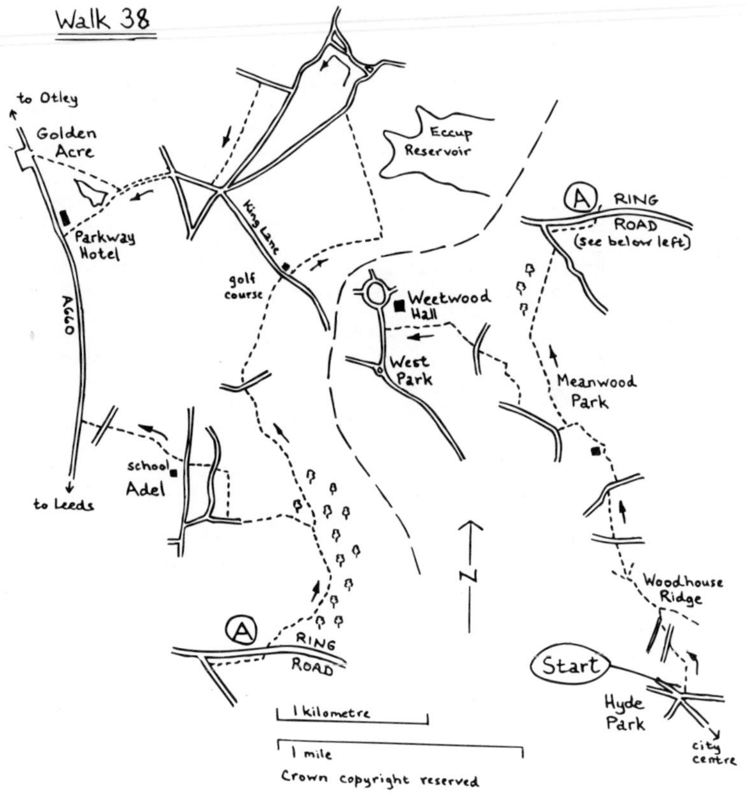

Walk 38
to Otley
Golden Acre
Parkway Hotel
A660
to Leeds
school
Adel
King Lane
golf course
Eccup Reservoir
Weetwood Hall
West Park
A RING ROAD (see below left)
Meanwood Park
Woodhouse Ridge
Start
Hyde Park
city centre
A RING ROAD
N
1 kilometre
1 mile
Crown copyright reserved

HYDE PARK TO WEST PARK, ADEL AND GOLDEN ACRE

WALK 38

3 miles (5 km) to West Park, 5 miles (8 km) to Adel, 7½ miles (12 km) to Golden Acre; Pathfinder 683 (SE23/33), 672 (SE24/34). A linear footpath route almost from the city centre to the countryside north of Leeds, largely along the valleys of Meanwood Beck and Adel Beck, a route also used by the Meanwood Valley Trail and the Leeds Dales Way Link.

By bus: *No. 1, 28, 55, 93, 96, 655, 755, 731, 780, 784 from the City Centre to Hyde Park.*
By car: *If you are intending to walk the whole route, it may be easier to park at Golden Acre on the A660 Leeds to Otley road, take the No. 780/784 bus to Hyde Park, then walk back to the car.*

From the traffic lights at Hyde Park keep the Hyde Park pub on your left and walk for a few yards along Woodhouse Street, but at the end of the pub building turn left between bollards along a paved path which soon bears right and joins a cobbled lane. When you reach a cross street continue forward up Cliff Lane. A yard or two after passing Grosvenor Park Gardens fork left along a narrow ginnel. Keep your line across the first street you meet and continue along the ginnel to a gap-stile, where you bear left for a few yards before turning right along Grosvenor Road. The large house at the end of the road is the residence of the Vice-Chancellor of the University of Leeds. But before you reach this look out for a gap in the high wall on the left and the continuation of the ginnel.

At the next street (Cumberland Road) bear right to find on the left at the end the final section of ginnel leading to Woodhouse Ridge. Bear left along the ridge with the valley of Meanwood Beck to your right. Drop gently to a junction of several paths and keep forward on the level middle path across the grass. At the far side descend a few steps, cross a track, climb a couple more steps and continue along the hedged path to Grove Lane. Cross straight over and follow the path to the next road (Monk Bridge Road). Cross this with care and turn right, but at the end of a field on the left turn left along a track. The large building which soon looms ahead was a tannery: bear right and then left round the end of it to find the continuation of the track, which soon narrows to a footpath between fences. Pass through a barrier onto a paved path and at the fork go left, with Meanwood Beck to your left and a cricket ground beyond.

The main route goes through a gap-stile on the right into Meanwood Park (see [*] below), but for West Park cross the white footbridge and another smaller one, after which the paved path ends. Turn right along the street (Hollin Drive) with houses on the left and the park on the right. Ignore the entrance into the park on the right by the pillar-box, and soon afterwards ignore a minor road forking right. The main road begins to curve left and climb, and just after a bungalow there is a stile by a gate on the right. Cross this and walk across the grass to another stile by a large gate opposite. Now you have a tall iron fence to your right. Cross the stile in the far corner of the field, bear right across a stone stile and continue along the fenced ginnel, which soon turns sharply left.

When you are faced by a gate ahead cross the step-stile on the right and bear left with a garden fence to your left to a tarmac lane. Cross this and follow the continuation of the footpath with a wood to the right and a garden to the left. Shortly you cross a stile onto Weetwood Lane. Cross and go right for a yard or two to find behind a pedestrian safety barrier a cobbled ascending walled ginnel. When you reach a tarmac access road cross straight over, cross the step-stile opposite and bear left along the track with the University sports grounds to your right. At a junction of paths keep forward along a paved path with lampposts, with a fence to the right. You reach the A660 between the West Park roundabout and the Ring Road.

[*] Turn right through the gap in the wall into Meanwood Park and follow the path between the picnic tables. When the path peters out keep forward to cross a tarmac cross path, then on over the grass to pick up a clear path which bears left towards the beck. Ignore the massive clapper bridge and keep the beck to your left. Ignore several more

bridges and soon you will pass through an arched gateway in a wall ahead, with a row of stone cottages up to your right. Turn left, cross the wooden bridge and turn right between stone gateposts, the beck now to your right. The path climbs a few steps and now you have an old mill goit to your left. If you crossed the next wooden footbridge on the left you would enter the Hollies, a public park with a fine display of rhododendrons and azaleas, but our route keeps forward.

At the next fork keep right to re-cross the beck by a footbridge at a weir; go left for a few yards, then right down some steps. Turn left along a clear cross track, shortly passing through a kissing-gate. The beck is to your left. Follow the path until you climb a few steps onto a road: cross this and bear left along the footway. A few yards before the Ring Road bear right along a signposted tarmac drive and where this turns right through a gate keep forward along the footpath, which soon bears left to pass through a tunnel under the Ring Road. Turn right up the steps and through the kissing-gate, soon crossing a stile into the woods, with Adel Beck to your right. When the path forks keep left round the outside edge of the woods, then cross a stile on the right and now the fence is on your left. At the next clear fork, keep left up the slope, and after some time the path bears right, now as a broad track through the wood. After 150 yards you reach a major fork: the main route keeps right (see [*] below), passing to the left of the Seven Arches aqueduct, but for Adel keep left.

Follow the track, at one point crossing over a cross track a few yards before you cross a disused cattle-grid, until you reach a tarmac road: bear left along it. In about 100 yards opposite an old stone house on the left turn right along a tarmac footpath with modern houses to the left and follow it round the outside edge of the houses, at first with grass then woodland to the right. At the far end of the wood fork right up a few steps and along a gravel path to the next road: cross it and go right for a few yards, then fork left up the steps towards a newsagent's shop. Pass in front of it, then turn left up a tarmac footpath and follow it to the next motor road. Adel Primary School is now to your left, but you cross the road and turn right for a few yards before entering a track on the left (look ahead to see part of the long causeway which gives this road its name). The track soon narrows to a footpath. Pass through a gateway and walk along the righthand edge of playing fields. Another gateway leads into a ginnel. Pass through a kissing-gate and walk along the track to reach Church Lane, Adel. Cross diagonally left and walk along Holt Close, a no through road. At the end a ginnel leads to the A660 opposite the Texaco garage.

[*] Pass to the left of Seven Arches, crossing the beck, and bearing slightly left uphill. Keeping always on the main path you will in time cross a clear cross path and drop to cross a shallow valley, climbing out of it by steps. Pass to the right of a small pond and bear right at the fork. Again keep to the main path. Just after walking along the lefthand edge of an open grassy area you are joined by a good track from the right: bear left along this to the next road (Stair Foot Lane), passing on the way a signposted path to Adel Crag, a short detour to a rocky eminence. Cross the road and take the path opposite, ignoring a minor path forking left in a few yards. Ignore another minor path forking right a few yards before a stile into a field. Cross this and bear right along the edge of the field. Ignore a gateway in the next corner and bear left with the field boundary. Cross a stile ahead in the next corner and keep on, soon with Headingley Golf Course to your left.

Cross straight over the next motor road (King Lane), passing to the right of the white-painted Golf Farm, along a track. When the track ends keep on with the hedge to your right and the golf course to your left. Cross a stile in the next corner and keep forward, soon with a fence to your left. A few yards before the far corner of this field, cross a stile on the left and walk at right-angles to your previous line, still with a fence to your left. Cross the stile in the far corner, and now there is a wood to your right with Eccup Reservoir beyond. Over the next stile keep forward on a clear path across the middle of the large field; near the far side the path keeps to the right of a hedge, which it follows to the next stile and road. Turn right along this.

The road drops into a dip and crosses a beck: take the left fork here. At the next junction go left again, and at the next one left again, and at the next one left again, now on a rather busier road. At the next junction turn right along Black Hill Lane. Near the end of the wood on the left take the signposted footpath into it. The clear path keeps close to the righthand edge of the wood (Eccup Whin). Shortly after the wood narrows you cross a stile: keep forward with a fence to your right, and follow it to a stile at the next motor road. Turn right along the road (King Lane again) and follow it to a T-junction: take neither of the roads here, but cross straight over and walk down the track signposted Meanwood Valley Trail. Either follow this track all the way to the A660 at the Parkway Hotel or fork right into Golden Acre Park and reach the main road through it.